blink-182 | Tales From Beneath Your Mom

By blink-182 with Anne Hoppus

books™

POCKET BOOKS

New York   London   Toronto   Sydney   Singapore

An *Original* Publication of MTV Books/Pocket Books

POCKET BOOKS, a division of Simon & Schuster, Inc.
1230 Avenue of the Americas, New York, NY 10020

ISBN: 0-7434-2207-4

First MTV Books/Pocket Books trade paperback printing
October 2001

10 9 8 7 6 5 4 3 2 1

For information regarding special discounts for bulk
purchases, please contact Simon & Schuster Special Sales
at 1-800-456-6798 or business@simonandschuster.com

Designed by Tim Stedman

Printed in the U.S.A.

This is for all
the people that
come to the
shows.

ANNE HOPPUS, sister of blink-182 bassist
Mark Hoppus, lives in San Diego, California.

Anne Hoppus wishes to thank:

Pete Ledesma and Skippy Fontaine for
reminding me of what it is I'm supposed to be
doing with my life.

And to Damon DeLaPaz for holding my hand
and my heart along the way (and for being
exceedingly patient during rewrites).

Special thanks also to Susan Raihofer and
the David Black Literary Agency, to everyone
at Pocket Books, and, of course, to
blink-182.

Introduction

I can't believe it's been ten years. I still think of blink-182 as being relatively new, though they've been with me through high school, college, and beyond.

The first time I met Tom I was a sophomore in high school. I was standing behind him in line to use the pay phone. I was calling Mom for a ride home. Tom had other reasons for using the phone. Eavesdropping on his conversation, I realized he was prankcalling a dental service. I glanced around, looking for his gaggle of giggling friends, his audience. But there was no one, Tom wasn't entertaining anyone but himself. He had waited in line and paid his money just to make himself laugh. I knew then that this was someone I needed to hang with. He had a Tony Hawk long-bangs, skater-punk haircut; a huge, ugly, olive green car; and no luck with the ladies. He was the only constant member of his first band, Big Oily Men, loved to draw phallic shapes (that's a nice way of putting it) on all of his classmates' papers as they were passed to the front of the room, and was above all an unceasingly loyal friend.

I don't remember meeting Mark, of course, but I do remember my big brother walking me to school in the mornings, building me an entire toy kitchen set with cardboard boxes, and making me cry a million times with the ol' "stop hitting yourself" trick. He completely embarrassed me in front of my prom date, and nursed me through every one of my heartbreaks, making me laugh when I thought I couldn't. I introduced Mark and

Tom in the summer of 1992. Mark had just recently moved to San Diego and was looking for someone to play music with. Tom complained to me every day that summer that all he wanted was his own band. It was only logical to bring the two together. I arranged a meeting one August night, and the rest is history.

I may be one of the selected few who has ever had the opportunity to witness love at first sight. There is no other way to describe it, though I am sure the guys would prefer I use a term with less of a homoerotic feel. That first August night, Mark and Tom played their guitars together for hours, the emerging tunes already bearing that distinctive blink-182 sound. Still, I probably would have been very bored that night if it hadn't been for the stupid jokes that were already being traded back and forth. And then, of course, Mark climbed the streetlight outside Tom's house, just to prove he could. He did make it to the top. It was the coming down that he wasn't so good at. Nothing serious, just a few weeks on crutches.

And Travis . . . It's never been clear if it was blink-182 that found him, or if he found blink-182. Either way, they found each other. What more could blink-182 ask for? In Travis, they found their better third—an exceptionally talented drummer, a good friend, and someone, thankfully, a little quieter than the other two members. You can't even joke about Travis—besides being a good percussionist, he is a good person, absolutely passionate about music and genuinely kindhearted.

For ten years now blink-182 has been the soundtrack to my life. They played at my high school grad night, until ordered to turn off. Apparently, they were disturbing the line dancers on the other side of the gym. In my little college dorm room, it was blink-182's original demo tape played over and over again that made me feel closer to home. I can still hear my roommate: "Did they just say 'The bitch has got four toes?'" Later, I even got suckered into selling T-shirts for the band on tour. For six weeks I lived with those bastards in very close quarters—sleeping on floors, driving through snow storms (and rain storms and tornado warnings), smelling unpleasant smells, pleading with all six kids who came out to the show to please just buy something! I wouldn't trade the experience for anything. Of course, I also wouldn't do it again, either.

I screamed the first time I heard a blink-182 song on the radio, and cried with pride when their second album went gold. I missed my friends when they were away on tour for months, worried about them, and waited for them to come home and entertain me.

I have watched as blink-182 has realized their dreams. They've come a long way from playing to an audience of three of our friends (and some unappreciative neighbors) in Tom's garage, to playing on stage to a sold-out crowd of 16,000 people at the Great Western Forum. From folding the covers of their first self-released cassette on my mom's living room floor, to signing a major label record deal and going on to multiplatinum sales. From van tours to bus tours. From "Who the hell are those loud obnoxious guys?" to "Ohmigod, it's blink-182." From juvenile fart jokes, to, well, juvenile fart jokes.

The journey hasn't always been an easy one. Mark, Tom, and Travis have all invested extraordinary amounts of time, energy, and heart. But easy or hard, the trip has always been incredible. I am thankful that I have had the opportunity to be a participant and a passenger. But, I am especially proud to call these boys my friends and my family. I cannot imagine my life without the excitement, the fun, and the laughter they have brought me.

Okay, this has got to stop. There is no way I am going to let myself get emotional over a bunch of retarded boys who never matured out of fourth grade! Oh yeah, poo poo, pee pee, boobies, wieners. Girls don't like me. Beings from outer space are living among us. Real funny. Great material. I can't believe I was getting teary eyed over the same guys that nicknamed one of their friends Shit Lips, and then forgot his real name. Come on, we're talking about blink-182 here. . .

And I love 'em.

"...take care
of your colon,
and your colon
will take care
of you."

—*blink-182*

"Hi, I'm Mark and I play bass and sing in blink-182. Tom and I started the band back in 1992 with nothing but a guitar, a bass, two penises, and smiles on our faces. And Tom loves men.

"Oh, yeah, by the way, I was born in Ridgecrest, CA, in March 1972 and I grew up there. I went to William Burroughs High School in Ridgecrest, and I wore eyeliner to school and kids made fun of me.

"Now I live in San Diego, and I'm married. And that's it."

1

"Hello, my name is Thomas Matthew Delonge, and I was born December 13, 1975. I'm a Sagittarius. Most people like me; they find me attractive. They also find me absolutely amazing in bed.

"I grew up in San Diego, CA, where I was born. I grew up skateboarding. That was my whole life. That and music. I got my first guitar for a birthday present when I was a freshman in high school. Then, I sat around and made my sister, Kari, and my brother, Shon, listen to songs about anything from zits to girls to food. And I tried to play Descendents' songs. I am the founding member of blink.

"But seriously, I am really good in bed."

"I guess we all know my name is Travis Barker. I was born 11-14-75 in Fontana, CA. I play the drums.

"I started playing drums when I was four, and quit when I was seven. Then I played piano for a while. I started drums again when I was seventeen. Now, I'm twenty-five and I still play drums. I played with the Aquabats for a while. And I joined blink-182 in 1998."

5

Tom Entertains Himself At Work

Tom is infamous for his tendency for practical jokes. When Tom still had a day job, he would often get bored, and would turn to pranks to keep himself entertained.

While these jokes included menial numbers such as the typical photocopying of the butt, prank phone calls, and using silly voices when dealing with customers, he was also known to pull off some really great ones. The most famous involved Tom, a phone call from mall security, and an innocent shopper.

The details: For a few months, Tom worked at a vitamin store in the mall. The shop was small, and often he would be the only person working.

One night, Tom had a brilliant idea. He placed a phone call to the frame shop across the hall. Tom told the clerk who answered the phone that it was mall security, calling to enlist the clerk's assistance in apprehending a known shoplifter. Tom could see the frame shop window from where he sat in the vitamin store. In describing the "shoplifter," Tom gave the store clerk a perfect description of a man he could see innocently window shopping outside the frame store. Security Guard Tom insisted that the clerk keep the "shoplifter" in the area, to stall him until mall security could arrive to make the arrest.

After hanging up, Tom just sat back and for twenty minutes watched as the civil-minded clerk stalled the man, harrassed him, almost physically grabbing him as he tried as hard as he could to keep the innocent "shoplifter" from leaving the area.

And, of course, mall security never showed up.

Tom quoting his mother's response to a blink show.

"I have never heard a person with such a foul mouth."

—Melody Maker, March 8-14, 2000

2 It all began with Big Oily Men. Which is to say, it all really began with Tom Delonge and his first band, an ever-changing lineup called Big Oily Men. This band was really just Tom on guitar and anyone else with a musical instrument who Tom could coax into playing music with him in his garage. Most people would not be familiar with the music of this band, though some Poway, California, residents may have seen the sheet of notebook paper taped to the back window of Tom's car with "Big Oily Men" written on it in permanent marker. This paper served as the only Big Oily Men sticker ever produced, the only Big Oily Men flier, and actually, the only material ever to be released by the band. This nonexistent band is important in the history of blink-182, however. It taught Tom two important lessons: One, he loved to play music. And, two, bands are

always better when they have members. The quest began.

Mark Hoppus was living in the wastelands of the California high desert in the small town of Ridgecrest, a place that celebrated every time a new stoplight was added to any of its twenty streets, a town four hours from anything that even resembled civilization. He played bass in a garage band called Of All Things with two of his friends. They played covers of influential punk bands like The Descendents and some original punk songs at parties, at bonfires held in the middle of the desert, and even scored a gig at the Oasis, the local music venue. But a small town like Ridgecrest just didn't have enough people to support a band—especially when half the population were creepy engineer types who worked on the Navy

8 base at the center of the town. The band found itself with no place to go. Mark himself found that Ridgecrest offered him few opportunities. He was looking for more out of life than what this small town had to offer. Plus, there were lots of snakes and spiders and scorpions and stuff in the desert. A person could get hurt. And, on top of that, it gets really, really hot.

Mark: "Thank God I left Ridgecrest because it was an awful city in the middle of nowhere."

So, in the summer of 1992 he left Ridgecrest for San Diego, a college education (that's what he told his parents anyway), and a job at a music store. Mark took his bass and his amp with him, but the band stayed behind. For a while, he tried to keep up with the band, returning to Ridgecrest on the weekends. But soon, Mark's manager at the music store just wouldn't give him the time off anymore. Maybe he started to get suspicious of Mark's cover story. Mark had told the manager that he worked with mentally disabled children in Ridgecrest and that he needed to have weekends off to attend their cute little plays and dinners. His manager had to start wondering how many damn plays these kids were going to make. With his work week filled with college-level human sexuality classes to fail, and the weekends filled with alphabetizing CDs and taking long lunch breaks at the music store, Mark's visits to Ridgecrest dried up, and Of All Things died. Mark missed the music almost immediately.

That might have been the end of the story

but for one significant event. An event that really pissed Tom's parents off at the time, but one that proved to be fortuitous. In 1992, Tom was kicked out of Poway High for attending a high school basketball game drunk. Tom tried

Tom, Kerry, and I spent a great deal of time together in the summer following Tom's semester at R.B.H.S. It was a typical summer: going to the beach, skateboarding, just hanging out listening to Tom's "clever"

> **"You know, what I remember most about being kicked out of Poway High was that it was the beginning of the second semester. We had just started our new classes, and me and my friend had decided to take aerobics for our P.E., 'cause it would be us and like sixty girls in tight clothes jumping around. Then, I got kicked out, so my friend got really pissed. He was like, 'Dude, you asshole, this shit's hard!' And he had to be in there all by himself."—Tom**

to explain that being drunk really made the game more exciting, but the administration just wasn't having it. He got the boot.

Expelled from Poway High and his aerobics class, Tom was forced to attend another local school for one semester. It was here, at Rancho Bernardo High, his new school, that Tom became friends with fellow skaterpunk Kerry Key, and consequently with Kerry's girlfriend, Anne Hoppus (That's me!). Can you see the plot beginning to develop? If you can't, well, geesh, keep reading. You'll figure it out eventually.

Tom: "Being kicked out of school was bad, but it was also the best thing in my life. Because none of us would be here today. blink-182 is one million percent around today because I got kicked out of school."

come-backs ("Hey, Delonge!" "Oh, I see you've seen me naked."). But this typical summer was marked by one constant: Tom's incessant complaining and whining. He really, really wanted a band. And he just would not shut up about it.

Mark was the same way. New to San Diego, he knew few people and often hung out with me, his little sister and good friend, to whom he, too, often complained about his lack of a band.

In a desperate attempt to shut the two up, and thinking that their mutual love of stupid jokes and pop-punk music might just be a good combination, I finally had to introduce Tom and Mark. And on a fateful night in August 1992, blink-182 came together for the first time. And, boy, did they suck.

"We had the same thoughts about songs, wrote songs about the same stuff, wanted songs to sound the same way. It was like somehow we were supposed to find each other and write music. Even today we'll get together and I'll show Tom something I've been working on, and he'll be like, dude, that sounds exactly like something I've been working on."—Mark

The two met in Tom's garage. Tom pulled out a red notebook in which he had written music and lyrics, probably when he should have been doing something else. Starting on page one, Tom and Mark explored all the songs Tom had written. Then, they played songs Mark had written. For hours, Mark and Tom played their guitars together. Even on that first night, the two started cowriting songs, songs that already sounded like the band that would be blink-182. A little known fact: "Carousel", the song that would eventually be a crowd favorite, actually found its beginnings that night in Tom's garage.

Tom: "Instantly, I felt like we had the exact same musical style; he just had it on a different instrument than me."

It was a match made in heaven. Once Mark and Tom met, they were never apart for long. Mark was still in school, but he arranged his schedule so that he only had classes two days a week. The rest of the time he was out with the boys, skating or practicing, or dressing up in costumes and terrorizing people at the grocery store. Most of it's on videotape, too. No joke at all, Mark and Tom were just made for each other. They had so much fun.

As Mark and Tom continued to practice together, they both knew they wanted to pursue the band as something more than just a way to kill a summer's night. And perhaps take their relationship itself to the next level, to finally become more than just friends. . . . The feelings were there, it was all just so confusing. . . . But, first things first. They needed a drummer.

Tom knew just the kid. Scott Raynor, at 14, was a heavy-metal kid with long hair and a penchant for Metallica.

Scott: "I met Tom at the Rancho Bernardo High Battle of the Bands. My band was playing and so was Tom. He sang 'Who's Gonna Shave Your Back Tonight?' acoustic to a crowd of hundreds. We started playing together—a strange mix of metal and Descendents-style punk which never seemed to click until Mark joined shortly after. Mark was the perfect bridge between Tom and me."

But when Tom saw him play at the R.B.H.S. Battle of the Bands, he realized that he was also a good drummer. He was in.

The practice sessions moved from Tom's garage (for which Tom's mom was eternally

grateful) to Scott's bedroom which had to be soundproofed for the sanity of Scott's family—a makeshift sort of soundproofing that involved covering the walls with empty egg cartons. (Everyone ate a lot of damn eggs for a while.) The equipment filled the room, leaving barely enough room for the musicians. Anyone who wanted to watch and listen had to sit under Scott's loft bed, which actually, was just a bunk bed with the bottom bunk removed. The practice sessions were hot, loud, and cramped. But no one ever cancelled. They always showed up. This was especially easy for Scott. After all, he lived there.

Tom: "Scott was always down for whatever with the band. He would do anything, go anywhere. He just needed a ride 'cause he was too young to get his license. I used to

"The hardest part was teaching Mark to sing like a man. He wanted everything to sound like a Barbra Streisand song."—Tom

have to drive him everywhere, and I gave him so much shit for it."

With a drummer, the band started to seem like more of a reality. They seemed closer than ever to actually being musicians. They all wanted to make this work. Mark, Tom, and Scott practiced everyday. They spent hours writing original music, hours trying to figure out what knobs to turn on their amps, hours trying to think of funny things to say when they had an actual show, and hours trying out different jumps to see which ones looked the coolest, often banging into equipment and/or band members in the crowded quarters.

It was during these many hours of work that the band briefly toyed with the idea of adding a singer to the group, finding a front man.

"I knew that with a singer, I could play more complicated guitar stuff," Tom remembers.

Mark does not remember. "See, this is why we need to write a book. I don't even remember this."

Tom: "If I was going to write a song, then I wanted to be able to sing it myself. And Mark and I were so compatible that we didn't need anyone else, really."

So, the band stuck with what they had. Mark and Tom would both sing, taking turns at slaughtering vocal patterns. Mark would play bass, Tom guitar, and Scott drums. The lineup was solidified.

The band officially became the most important thing in all three members' lives. Which didn't sit well with Mark's girlfriend. (Did we

"My girlfriend and I were living in this really crappy basement apartment. We had barely enough money to pay rent. I had money in savings, and I went out one day and bought equipment. I bought a new amp and a new bass cabinet. I was so stoked because it was the first professional equipment I ever had. But all I remember is coming home and having her just yell at me. She was pissed that I had spent money on something we didn't need. I just kept telling her that this was what mattered to me, this was my life. But she said, no, you have to choose. Me or the band. And she lost."—Mark

forget to mention her?) Jealous of the amount of time dedicated to things that were not her, she demanded that Mark make a choice. It was her or the band.

While his girlfriend did eventually lose, Mark at first did decide to leave the band. But a few days later, when Tom told him that he and Scott had borrowed a four track and were going to record a tape, Mark knew he'd made the wrong decision. He wanted to be back in the band.

Tom: "I saw in Mark's face how bummed he was that we would be doing that without him. At that point, he just made a choice for himself, regardless of what his girlfriend thought. He got stubborn, and he came back. But he had to go through the whole interview process again, you know. I mean, he can't just expect to walk right back into his old job."

Besides that brief lapse of judgment on Mark's part, there was no question that the band came before anything. This was to be their lives. Blink-182 was officially born— only, then, they called themselves Duck Tape. And they had the cutest little duck mascot. This name lasted only a few days. Ever fickle, Tom announced only a short while later that he much preferred the name blink. This name stuck. And they had the cutest little bunny mascot. Which was an obvious choice—nothing is more closely associated with the punk scene than cute little bunny rabbits.

It was now early 1993. The band had a line-up. They had songs. They had a style.

15

16 They had a name. They had a bunny.

They took everything they had and brought it into Scott's bedroom to record the four-track whose promise had reminded Mark of what really mattered to him.

The resulting recording, if you can call it that, was dubbed *Flyswatter*.

Mark: "I thought it would be cool to name it *Flyswatter*. It doesn't mean anything, it just sounded cool. And I took color copies of a modern-art-type drawing I did, and that was the artwork."

Flyswatter was actually little more than a collection of sloppy original songs with a few covers thrown in. The songs were recorded live with no mixing or anything that actually makes recordings sound good. Then, Tom ran

off a few copies not knowing how this would haunt him in later years. (Damn you, eBay!) Tom sold a few copies to kids at school during lunch. Then, production ceased.

As awful as the tape was, it must have helped. After sending out a few copies of it, blink landed their first shows.

The very first blink show was on a Tuesday night at a 21+ venue called the Spirit Club. It wasn't so much a venue as it was just a bar that sometimes allowed bands to play. There was no guaranteed payment. Bands were given tickets to sell. On the night of the show, the band would return whatever tickets they hadn't sold. They were allowed to keep the money from the tickets they did sell. On the night of their first show, blink returned all of the tickets they had been given to sell.

Tom: "We didn't know anyone who was over twenty-one. We weren't even twenty-one. We couldn't even go inside until it was time for us to play. We had to sit outside all night."

Mark: "There was nobody there. It was us, our friend Cam, who was the only person we knew who was old enough to go to a bar,

Tom: "They were weird, they had this lighting rig, but it was all put together with like Q-tips and duct tape and coat hangers. And they got really mad at me 'cause I screwed it up when we were playing. I don't even remember how."

Beyond that, the promoters were total jerks to blink and to their friends. And Tom

"Kids are always asking me where they can find a copy of Flyswatter. I always think, dude, if you even knew what you were trying to get. It's like trying to collect an actual piece of feces. It's just a four-track recording done in a bedroom. We couldn't sing or play. You can't even hear anything on the recording. It's awful."—Tom

one biker guy who was already drunk, and the bartenders. That was it. And for some reason I was still nervous."

The second blink show was an after-hours in-store performance at the now defunct Alley Kat Records in downtown San Diego. There were two bands on the bill. Blink was the opener. The other band was an awful, hardcore gothic band whose name no one even remembers. The crowd for both bands was only about ten people. And all ten people were friends who had come to support blink. Blink had fliered all of the local high schools. The headliners didn't have a single person. Despite this obvious lack of fans, the gothic band ridiculed blink as being garage-band kids and proceeded to set up a very elaborate light show to accompany their songs.

shocked himself on the microphone while playing, sending his lips into unattractive spasms right in front of the girl he liked. The night certainly didn't have a rock-and-roll glamorous feel to it.

But who cared. They were a band, they had a tape, and they were finally playing shows. The guys were stoked. And after those first two disasters, the shows became somewhat more frequent. Poway High students, who already loved Tom, and had, in fact, elected him Homecoming King (GO TITANS!), were beginning to take an interest.

The guys were proud of what they had accomplished. Since forming in the summer of 1992, they had written songs, learned to play them with only a few mistakes, and had performed in front of actual people. And they had the balls to record these early songs and let people hear them. All of that, in only about a year of even knowing each other. Their careers had begun. They would grow and change. Eventually Scott would be replaced in the lineup by Travis Barker. Most of the early songs written in these days were lost to history. Future shows and recordings increased in both quantity and quality. But, despite the years that have passed since these early days, the boys who first played crappy music in Tom's garage and then in Scott's bedroom are the same boys who play on arena stages today. They came together whining, complaining, and sucking. And today they continue to do the same.

Mark Has Tourrett's. Or At Least Acts Like

He's doing much better at controlling himself now, thanks for asking. But not so long ago he used to have these weird attacks. Ask anyone who knows him. He would get this look in his eye, and those in the know would run. They knew something messy was most likely going to happen.

In one of his episodes, Mark crushed a economy-size bag of tortilla chips and then swung the bag around his head, spraying chips all over the room and everyone in it. He had a similar incident involving a bottle of orange juice.

At home, instead of taking a nice clean slice of the whipped-cream-based cake his mom had made, Mark scooped most of the cake into his hand and proceeded to smear it all over his face and chest. After a few minutes and handfuls, the cake coated Mark and a lot of the kitchen. Of course, that was when Mom walked in. Mark simply explained that he had spilled the cake. He has similar smearing problems when it comes to shaving cream.

Mark has no idea where these attacks come from, or why they happen. He says usually he just gets bored, has an idea of something that would be funny, and then is overwhelmed by this compulsion to act on his thoughts. Crazy.

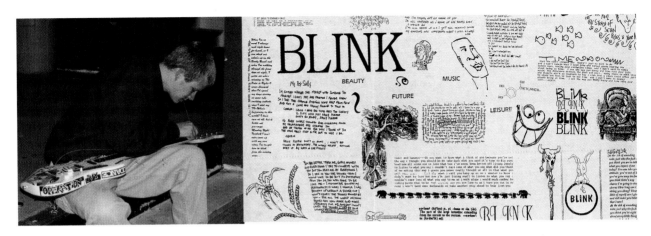

"Future Proctologists of America camp."
—Where the band met, according to an official blink-182 bio

"Naked skydiving."
—How the band met, according to Tom

3 Blink's first shows weren't so good. But so what. Blink had played several shows since then. The audience was still mostly friends, but that was beginning to change. In addition to whatever parties blink could scrounge up, they had also found their way onto the bill as the opening band for other local acts at Soma, San Diego's main all-ages venue. At this time, Soma was still in downtown San Diego in its original location on Market Street. Big-name acts like NOFX and Green Day played on the main floor, while smaller acts were relegated to the basement, an area lovingly referred to as "the Dungeon." The Dungeon was a dark, boxy room with the stage only about a foot higher than the floor. There was little room on stage to move, and only slightly more room for the crowd. There was only one rule in the Dungeon, which was

that the pit had to stay between the four posts that framed the stage. This rule was usually kept. Mostly because few bands down there attracted a large enough crowd to spread any further than was allowed. In the Dungeon, even the headliners were usually small local acts, with even smaller bands opening. Blink was one of these even smaller bands.

The early Dungeon shows were about as far removed from the more recent arena tours as a band can get. The band's equipment would be piled into the back of the "Family Truckster," Mark's mom's big, blue station wagon. This was not the kind of vehicle these young punk kids wanted to be seen in driving to a show, but it was the only one they had that was big enough to hold their equipment. At the club, Mark, Tom, and Scott would wrestle the heavy equipment down the stairs that lead to the Dungeon and stash it in an unprotected corner as they waited for their turn to play. A crowd of thirty to forty people was a huge turnout. Many of the kids who came out had come to see the other bands. Only a few would watch blink, and those few were mostly friends.

Mark: "I remember always being afraid that I would hit my head on the ceiling above the

seriously. They needed to headline their own Dungeon show and get a lot of people to come out. To be considered for even an opening slot on the main floor, blink had to prove that they were a band that could draw a large crowd. They needed a hundred people, and then they'd be set. If one hundred people would come to a show and say "blink" at the door, they'd finally be able to play the main floor at Soma. That would be big-time. But how the hell do you get one hundred people

"Tom was just hyper. He always has been. He just wouldn't sit still, especially when it came to the band. In the beginning, it was always Tom who was pushing us."—Mark

20

stage because it was so low. But it was always awesome to play anyway. The Dungeon was awesome. It's cool to have a venue that gives small bands a chance, bands that only draw ten or twenty or thirty people."

Tom: "Playing the Dungeon was great. I can totally remember sitting outside the club being so stoked to be playing a real show at a real club. But I was bummed, too, because I knew that in an hour the night would be over, and we might have to wait another month to play there again."

But as happy as the guys were playing the Dungeon, they also wanted to know what it felt like to play the big shows, to play upstairs. But first, they would have to prove to Soma that they were a band to take

you don't know to like you enough to admit it to a bouncer at a club? Unfortunately, all three of the blink guys together could not dig up one hundred friends. They were lucky to come up with the ten or so that were blink show regulars. Either they needed to find more friends (never gonna happen), or they had to get their name out. They needed more shows to get more shows.

Tom was on it. While all three wanted the band to succeed, in the early days it was Tom who was truly driven. He was willing to do whatever it took to make this band happen. Tom brought a tape recorder to practice on a regular basis and made tapes to send out to promoters at clubs across San Diego. He called these promoters to the point of stalking them, begging for any slot on any show. He called local high schools, telling the

SIDESHOW

SOMA
L·I·V·E

SATURDAY, APRIL 9

PAPILLON
BLINK
PRODUCT
GRIP
FORMERLY FUSS BUDGET
LOOPHOLE

$5 • 5305 Metro Street • Doors Open 8:00

Located where Freeway 8 and 5 meet. Take Morena Blvd. to
Linda Vista Road. Go one block. Turn left on Metro.

For more info 239-SOMA • ALL AGES

principals that blink was a motivational band with a strong antidrug message. Could blink play a show at their school during lunch or an assembly? Tom was tireless and had no shame when it came to working his band.

Tom: "I wanted to play all the time. I would be at work, but I'd be on the phone calling people. I used to put up fliers at school just saying, 'Hey, we're a band.' I sent out a million tapes. God, I just loved to have shows."

Hyper, shameless stalker, or whatever, it worked. Blink played shows regularly. And with the shows came people. More and more, blink became a recognized name in the San Diego music scene as people had the opportunity to hear them play nearly every weekend. Blink also had the advantage of being a band that stood out in San Diego. In the

mid-nineties, San Diego was known for its heavier rock-style bands, with popular artists like Rocket from the Crypt and Fluf leading the pack. A snot-nose, politically incorrect band of skater kids who talked about farts and wieners between fast punk songs was bound to get some attention. And blink definitely got attention. Finally, there were faces in the crowd that no one recognized. Lots of them.

Blink never would have their chance to play the main floor at the Market Street Soma, but not for their lack of one hundred people. Before they had the opportunity to reach that long-coveted stage, the original Soma closed its doors and relocated. The new Soma substituted a side stage for the Dungeon, but the concept remained the same.

I'll be there-
what's your excuse?

BLINK
friday june 17th
at
soma
with: loophole
driptank
and –
the muffs
show starts at 8:00 p.m.

22 Soon after the reopening, blink headlined their own show on the side stage. They had worked long and hard to reach this point, and they spread the news of their show to anyone and everyone they could reach. Soma was THE place to play in San Diego.

Mark: "Soma was like home away from home. All the punk kids who didn't give a fuck about football games and proms or whatever came to hang out at Soma. All the losers went there to see their friends, check out a band. Every weekend they'd come out. It was always rad to play Soma."

On the night of their first headlining show, blink owned Soma. The crowd of losers was all theirs. The small side-stage area was packed with kids, and when blink started to play, the entire crowd moved.

Tom: "The kids were coming in, and I didn't recognize half of them. And they just kept coming and coming. We had something like 140 kids that night. It was scary. I mean, that was our show. Those kids came to see US! I was scared shitless that we were going to play bad or something."

But blink didn't play badly. They had a great show. Between fast, loud, catchy pop punk songs, Mark and Tom joked back and forth about masturbation and poop and, of course, girls. It was half concert, half Night at the Improv. It was just like they were in Tom's bedroom but add 140 screaming punk rockers. All these unfamiliar faces just ate it up. The place went crazy. There wasn't a safe corner to hide in. As the crowd pushed forward, the people in the front were pushed up the three steps and onto the "stage." Mics were

> **"We were a brand new band, really. And we were kids still. We had all dreamed of being in a band, and there we were actually doing it. Everything back then felt huge. We didn't care if we played to ten people or one hundred or whatever. We were just having so much fun doing it at all. Maybe that helped, maybe just doing it for the fuck of it was the right way to do things, because everything just kept going up."—Mark**

knocked over. The band could hardly move with the extra bodies on stage. It was totally punk. It was awesome. And they got their one hundred people. The main stage was finally, and deservedly, theirs.

Their first big show on the main floor was on a Thursday night opening for Face to Face.

Tom: "It was insane. We thought we'd made it."

Now blink could legitimately claim a following. But bigger things just kept coming.

In 1993 and 1994, blink kept playing, and playing, and playing. They could be found on stage almost every weekend, either as a headliner on the Soma side stage, an opener on the main stage, or at any one of the few other small all-ages venues that dotted

San Diego County. (Anyone remember the Soul Kitchen in El Cajon? That strip-mall club next to the sex shop where the bands played in the window display area and most of the crowd sat on couches? Blink played there a couple of times.) Even YMCA centers and Elks Lodges. The only place a fan couldn't catch blink was at the 21+ clubs, bastions of the gasoline jacket-wearing rockers. Despite blink's growing popularity, these clubs still turned a cold shoulder to the band. This was fine with blink. Besides being technically illegal for the still-underage trio, 21+ shows never had the energy all-ages crowds had. The kids were always a better crowd. Blink was more than happy to stick with them.

In just a few years, blink had come a long way from Tom's garage. They were a "real"

23

"We were the kids we were playing to, you know. I mean, we were going to school, trying to get girls, goofing around. It's what we sang about and what we did, and it's what the kids in the audience were doing. I think that's why people liked us. They knew us."—Tom

24 band now. They had shows and they had fans. Now, they wanted an album. A real one, something not recorded in Scott's bedroom.

Mark was still working at the record store, if you could call what he did working. His manager, Pat Secor, had an honest love for music. He had taken the job running this record store because he wanted to learn more about the business side of music. When Mark was not too busy watching the in-store TVs (never allowed), eating his FunDip (no food on the sales floor), sporting his T-shirt (no shirts without collars), baseball cap (no hats), and blue hair (no unnatural hair colors), and ignoring customers, he and Pat would talk about the music world.

Mark: "My friend Pat, who was also my manager at the music store, listened to the same music that I did, and we would talk all the time. He wanted to start his own label, and we wanted to put out a demo tape. So he was like, hey, I'll front you the money, and we'll split the profits until you pay me back. So, with some of his money, and some of ours, we went into the studio."

Scott: "Pat was the first person to have faith in us."

This demo tape became known as *Buddha.* It was recorded at Doubletime Studios in Santee, California. Jeff Forrest, "the coolest guy with the worst hair ever" according to Mark, engineered the album, doing the best he could with only three nights of studio time and an extremely laughable "budget." On top of that, Mark was supersick and everything had to be arranged and rearranged around school and work schedules. But they did it. They recorded their first release.

Tom: "I remember we were super stoked on the sound-effects tape they had at the studio. We recorded in like three nights and still took a couple of hours to add in applause and laughter and stuff from the sound effects tape because we thought it would sound so funny."

For the cover art, well, it was really just color copies of photographs taken by good friend Cam Jones. Mark and Cam spent an afternoon together taking "artsy" photographs in and around Scott's backyard. The Buddha in the photos had been a present from Mark's stepfather. Mark just thought it looked cool and grabbed it on the way to Scott's for the photos. When the pictures were developed, Mark and Cam took the photos to a copy shop to run off color copies. Together, they cut and pasted and rearranged until they liked them the way it looked. The lyric sheets were the same breed— handwritten and photocopied a thousand times. It was definitely an amateur release.

But as in all recordings, it is the songs that ultimately make it or break it. And these songs were great. Mark and Tom, as unlikely as their easygoing personalities made it seem, took songwriting very seriously. It was the one point upon which the band strove for perfection.

Mark: "The songs were definitely what mattered. It was the only goal we ever really set for ourselves as a band. To write great songs. We might not play every show perfectly, we might not hit every note right, we might not have the best performance, but we had good songs."

Tom: "I think it's been really big that we are a band that kids can relate to. We write about stuff that every kid knows. But it was almost as important to make people laugh. At the end of *Buddha* we spent more time getting our joke songs right than the other songs. Songs about my mom being a trans- vestite and having sex with our families or whatever. But we still got the other songs done."

Some of these "other" songs remain favorites of the band. And of fans. Years after the demo was originally recorded, the songs were strong enough to attract the interest of Kung Fu Records who finally released the album in CD format and for the first time made it widely available.

But in the days before blink even understood what distribution was, getting the demo to their fans took a lot more work. Mark or Tom would drive to one place to pick up the cassettes—actual cassettes in one box, cas- sette cases in another. Then, they would drive to the copy shop to run off more copies of the liner notes and lyric sheets. Then, to Mark's house, where the whole family (yes, OKAY! Mark still lived at home, there's nothing wrong with that) would spend hours watching TV. Well, that was pretty normal.

25

26 What was different is that, in these days while watching those hours of TV the family would also be folding and combining pieces and parts until a complete blink *Buddha* cassette emerged. For a nice crisp crease on lyric sheets, we recommend sitting on the paper. Try it. Anyway, once the cassettes were together, some would be loaded into Mark's car and delivered to the various record stores around town that would take consignment.

Mark: "I totally remember driving around to all the record stores to drop off tapes to sell. I'd go to Lou's Records, and Off the Record, and Music Trader. It was so cool because the tapes were actually selling, that's why I had to keep going back every week. Music Trader would have sold one copy, Off the Record sold two, or whatever. But that meant that people were actually walking into a music store and buying something that we had written and recorded. It was awesome."

The tapes were also selling at blink shows. Fast. Old fans wanted a copy to play in their cars. New fans wanted a chance to give what they had just heard another listen. Whatever the motive, kids wanted the tapes. More and more often, Mark and Tom were making the trip to the cassette plant to pick up another box, then another box. They couldn't believe it.

In addition to their brisk cassette market, blink was also selling T-shirts now. Tom and Mark bought a silkscreen and set up shop in Mark's mom's garage. Soon, they were churning out T-shirts. Not the nice, professional, high-quality T-shirts the bigger bands offer. No, these were crappy homemade blink shirts with chunks missing from the designs and smeared lettering.

They would print enough shirts to take to an upcoming show, and then they would scour the house for anything else that would hold the ink. Pillowcases, sheets, boxer shorts—whatever was available. The entire odd assortment was hung to dry while the guys cleaned out the screen and started all over again with another design. The place would reek of ink and bleach for days. This would have been the perfect time for Mark or Tom to commit a crime. Neither had fingerprints for a while—the silkscreen chemicals had burned them off. But it was pretty damn cool to have T-shirts.

Mark: "Our T-shirts were so funny back then. They didn't even really make sense. There would be a cool-looking drawing on the front or something, and then on the back it would say something like 'Teenage Tit

Freaks.' I have no idea what we were thinking. We'd get special orders from some of our friends, like, hey could you please leave the tit freaks off of my shirt please?"

Even with the Teenage Tit Freak thing, the T-shirts were selling. Sure, they weren't selling thousands, or even hundreds. But that really didn't matter. The fact that one kid liked blink enough to wear a shirt that said "Teenage Tit Freak" on the back was enough for them. That was incredible.

The band seemed solid to Mark, Tom, and Scott. It had become almost their entire lives. But they were about to be reminded that other forces also could affect their band, with good and bad results. Just when the band had really come together, Scott's parents sold their house in Poway and relocated to Reno, Nevada, taking their still high-school-aged son with them. Blink had lost their drummer. They replaced Scott briefly with friend and musician Mike Krull, but the band felt wrong without Scott. After a few months, they saved their money and began flying Scott out for shows. Eventually, Scott would convince his parents to allow him to move back to San Diego to live with Mark's family. The band was whole again, and they continued their string of successes.

Scott: "The summer I lived with Mark and his family was probably the greatest summer of my life so far. I left home at 17, came to San Diego, we bought a van, finished our first video... I had all kinds of dreams in my head and they were all coming true."

And Mark, Tom, and Scott weren't the only ones who noticed their success. They were about to encounter the good that came from outside forces.

When You Fight, The Only Person You Hurt Is Yourself.

At a headlining show at the Palace in Los Angeles, members of blink-182 and their stage crew noticed one of the bouncers using excessive force on a kid in the crowd. Actually, the bouncer was punching the kid in the face.

While Mark stood on stage and spewed expletives at the bouncer, Stage Manager Stuart picked up a heavy roll of duct tape and lobbed it at the bouncer's head. He missed, the tape hit a monitor, and flew back up on stage to hit Tom squarely in the face.

During another altercation with a overly ambitious bouncer, Mark went a little far with the verbal insults. After the show, the bouncer and some of his bouncer friends came looking for Mark to even the score. Mark saw them coming and promptly ran out the back of the venue, jumping into the first car he saw, and demanding the surprised fan inside drive him to safety. Mark left Tom and Scott behind, trying to explain to some very angry, very big men that they had nothing to do with Mark's big mouth.

"In Southern California, mom jokes are always the worst thing to do with your friend. You go, 'I fucked your mom last night,' so we've just taken it to a different level. We say, 'We fucked our own moms,' it's mom joke hara-kiri. You do it to yourself. It's a sacrifice you make for a laugh."

—Tom Delonge

4 In the early days of blink, San Diego, also known as "The Next Seattle," had a thriving music scene, and at the heart of that scene was the local independent record label, Cargo Records.

Every band's dream is a record deal. Cargo Records was about to make that dream come true for blink.

On the record-deal front, blink had two allies working for them. Brahm Goodis was a skater-punk kid whose friends had turned him on to blink. His father was Eric Goodis, president of Cargo Records. Brahm knew his father wanted to diversify the label, to incorporate more diverse styles of music. Brahm thought blink and their style of Southern California punk fit the diversification bill perfectly and encouraged his father to listen to a tape.

Also pulling for blink was O, guitarist for Fluf. Fluf was huge in San Diego, and they were also the cornerstone band for Cargo Records, so O had a certain amount of influence in the San Diego music scene. O saw potential in blink and pushed for them right from the beginning. Together, O and Brahm finally got through to Eric Goodis, convincing him to check out a blink show. The record-deal wheels began to turn.

The first time Mark, Tom, and Scott walked into the Cargo Records offices they were completely intimidated.

Mark: "We were immature punk kids in a band, and now, here we were in an office with ringing phones and actual desks with people who sat behind them and did nothing but work music all day."

"Eric Goodis made a bet when he signed us. He said we'd only sell 3000 copies. Now, here we are nearing 250,000 sold. We won that bet."— Tom

30 Eric Goodis sat the three down in his office and made the band an offer. *Buddha* sales were strong; the tape had gone from being a sometime seller to a strong hit in the local scene. But Eric wanted to start small and Cargo Records offered to release a seven inch with blink. Even though they were intimidated, blink was smart enough to know that this was not what they wanted.

Blink had already set their sights on releasing a full-length CD. With or without a label, they were prepared to do just that. They had saved some money and made arrangements with a friend from another local band to record and release one on their own if need be. Unwilling to lose blink, when Eric heard this, he withdrew his original offer, and Cargo Records agreed to sign blink on a trial basis.

Holy crap. Blink had a record deal.

Mark: "We were so excited, I don't even think any of us read the contract. They handed it to us, and it was like, 'Cool. We'll take it.' I know we didn't have a lawyer or anyone look over it. We were too stoked to think about anything but signing before someone got smart and took it away."

They took the contract and they signed, no questions asked. Well, technically, Mark was the only member of the band who actually signed the contract. Scott was still a minor and couldn't legally enter into any agreement. And on the day the contract was due, Tom was working at his job delivering huge bags of cement and could not be found. Anxious to complete the deal, Mark had a friend, uhh, fill in as Tom and sign his name

to the contract. No one at Cargo seemed to notice that Tom's signature looked a little girly, or that his signature never looked quite that feminine again.

The deal had hardly been completed before the blink guys headed for the studio. This time they were to record in Los Angeles, at the famous Westbeach Studios. Mark and Tom were beside themselves with excitement.

Mark: "This was hallowed ground. It was like going into church or something. Some of the greatest punk bands in the world had recorded there—Bad Religion, NOFX, Face to Face, Ten Foot Pole. We were in total awe."

To add to the sense of awe, Tom would actually record through Bad Religion guitarist Mr. Brett's amp. The entire band felt somehow connected to genius. They felt even more

connected when they accidentally broke one of Mr. Brett's microphones. Oops. The studio was too nice to ask this poor young band to replace the expensive equipment.

Mark: "I don't know what the hell we were thinking. The three-day schedule hadn't worked out so good with *Buddha* and now we were trying it again with a real CD."

Blink only reserved the studio for three days, they were once again recording under serious time constraints.

Mark, Tom, and Scott were unfamiliar with Los Angeles, and as they made their way to the studio for the first day of recording, they got lost. Terribly lost. Three-hours-late-to-the-studio lost. Once they found the studio, they got to work immediately, setting up Scott's drums and starting to lay down tracks.

"You couldn't even move. That bed was awful. I was way too close to my bandmates for those few days. All night we slept together in the same bed, and then we'd all climb into my truck and drive to the studio three across. People must have really wondered about us." —Tom

32 Despite the lost time, and the pressure of limited resources, the recording went well.

Mark: "We really wanted to make a good record. We were working ten- to twelve-hours straight, hardly even breaking for food or anything. And the people that were there helping us were awesome."

O, blink's friend from Fluf, was producing, and the entire studio crew was giving their all to make this album good. Steve from Ten Foot Pole was a constant figure in the studio, hanging out and helping when he could. And, contrary to popular belief, he did NOT eat all of blink's chips.

Mark: "That was totally cool to have Steve from Ten Foot Pole there. I loved his band, and now here he was helping me with my band, telling us he liked our stuff. It meant a

whole lot for some reason."

Tom: "The thing that I remember most about recording *Cheshire Cat* was one of the engineers. His name was Steve, not from Ten Foot Pole, a different Steve. When he ate, he ate on the floor on his hands and knees with his butt in the air. It was really weird."

After a long day of work, the band headed to the hotel room for some much-needed sleep. They had made reservations at a hotel not far from the studio for a room with two double beds. They didn't know that the hotel they had reserved was a fucking nightmare, worst-case-scenario dive. After weaving their way through the crackheads and prostitutes that were gathered outside the lobby, blink checked in and discovered that they did not

The Meaning Behind 182

There actually is no meaning behind 182. It's a completely random number. But in interviews over the years Mark and Tom have gotten a little creative. Here are some of their explanations:

• Mark's ideal weight.

• The number of miles between Mark's house and his girlfriend's.

• The number of Mark's grandpa's race car.

• The number of Mark's grandpa's boat in World War II.

• The number of times Al Pacino says the F-word in *Scarface*.

• The eighteenth letter of the alphabet is *R*. The second is *B*. 18 + 2 = RB, or Rancho Bernardo where Mark and Scott lived for years.

34   have two double beds as requested. They had one king-size bed. After working for twelve hours, Mark, Tom, and Scott had to sleep three across in one bed. All three nights they slept in that bed. Tom had terrible nightmares about cross-country skiing. He kept pushing and pushing with his two poles, but he never got anywhere. He woke up still tired. On the contrary, Mark and Scott kept waking up in great moods, with huge smiles on their faces.

Miracle of miracles, the CD was finished in only three days. Looking back, blink can hear the evidence of it only taking three days in the quality of the recording. But at the time, it was near perfect to the band. The album included several songs that had originally appeared on the *Buddha* demo as well as several new songs that were even better. These new songs were fast, upbeat, and well, just

plain good. And they were all together on one CD that a kid could really buy in stores. How rad was that.

Mark: "We recorded *Cheshire Cat* and it's a cool album. I think the songs on that album are great. I would love if the recording were better, but at the time we didn't have the money to get more time or to do anything different. We couldn't afford it. We just wanted to get a CD out. And that's what it took to get it out."

The CD was called *Cheshire Cat* after the mad cat from *Alice in Wonderland*. The cover featured a Siamese cat with intensely colored eyes. The cat photo came from a calendar a salesman had left at Tom's warehouse. The band asked permission to use the photo, but the calendar company declined the

request. Unwilling to take no for an answer, blink employed Cargo's art department to computer enhance the photo until the band was safe from copyright infringement.

It was official. Blink had their first real CD. And they were soon to have their first radio play. "M&Ms" was a song that hit a special chord with fans, and with 91X radio deejay Mike Halloran. When Mike made the song a regular part of his radio show playlist, he became the first deejay in the world to play blink on the radio. (Mark would like to point out, "A lot of people like to claim they were the first to play us. We hear that all over the country. But it's not true. It was Mike from 91X.")

When Mark, Tom, and Scott heard their song on the radio for the first time, they freaked.

"I wanted the M&Ms video to be fifty guys lined up, and have us shooting at their nuts. Just a whole video of slo-mo close-ups of these guys' nuts exploding. But I guess that was too expensive. So, we did this instead." —Tom

36 For Mark, it was a moment just like in the movie *That Thing You Do.* Tom was in his car when he heard it, and rolled down his window, yelling at everyone to turn their damn radios on.

Tom: "I even yelled at people on bikes. Silly me, they don't usually have radios. But I didn't care, 'cause, damn them, I had a song on the radio!"

The band's success continued when Cargo offered the band a small budget to film a music video. "Small budget" being a key phrase. Most videos cost at least a half million dollars. "M&Ms" would be shot for under $10,000. Darren Doane, who had previously worked with MxPx and Pennywise, directed the video, and did a damn good job. It followed a basic storyline.

All three members wake up in the morning with their girlfriends. Each band member steals something from the girls. Then they sneak out of their homes to meet and go run around at Belmont Park and act like idiots. Finally, they head to Soma for a show, where the slighted girlfriends are waiting for them. A gunfight ensues. The guys fight their way onstage only to realize that the show had been postponed, ha ha!

Mark: "It's totally the things like filming a video that make you feel like you have hit the big time. We weren't planning on doing anything with that video except hoping it got on a surf video or something, but I still felt like a rock star that day. I mean, we hired models! We paid for models to hang out with us all day!"

38 The video did make it onto a surf video, or two, and was included on several video compilations. A misguided Cargo Records employee even presented the video to MTV where the execs threw the tape out at first sight of the girls with guns. Blink was banned from MTV.

With a base of loyal fans, radio play, and a banned video, *Cheshire Cat* was a strong seller. Kids all around the country were buying the CD. For the first time, blink wasn't just a local San Diego band, this irreverent trio was creating a buzz nationwide. And, they caught the attention of Rick DeVoe.

Rick DeVoe grew up in the SoCal surf-punk scene, going to parties, checking out the new bands. He loved the punk music world, and even when it came time to grow up, he refused to leave it. He took his passion for music and turned it into a career, first as one of the most respected punk promoters in America and later one of the most respected punk managers. In San Diego, he started a promotion company called Big Dummy under the umbrella of Bill Silva Presents. Rick was the first to promote The Offspring and he was close friends with Pennywise. He was also managing San Diego's own Unwritten Law. And now, he was calling Mark's house. It appeared he wanted to manage blink, too.

Blink could not believe their luck. Tom threw together a "press kit" for Rick that was little more than photocopies of fanzines, blink reviews, and some blink cartoons that Tom had drawn.

Tom: "I was praying we could do shows with this guy; he was this rad punk promoter who did these awesome shows with The Offspring, NOFX, and Pennywise. He did all the huge punk shows. I so wanted him to put us on a show."

The band crossed their fingers and hoped their luck would hold. It did, and Rick signed on with blink for the long haul.

It was a perfect match. Rick and blink were made for each other. While Rick was an admired member of the music industry, he was also the by-product of a surf-punk adolescence—a loser just like the blink kids. Rick and blink were immediate friends. He took the band on when they were nobodies. He swore he would take the band as far as he possibly could. To this day, he is the band's best friend, hardest worker, and strongest ally. Thank God for Rick DeVoe.

Soon after Rick DeVoe came onboard, he brought the band to the attention of their other guardian angel, Rick Bonde of the Tahoe Agency. The Tahoe Agency, owned and operated by husband-and-wife team Rick and Jean Bonde, was a booking agency based out of Lake Tahoe that worked with such big names from the punk and ska world as Sublime and Skanking Pickle. Rick Bonde believed in blink right from the start. He volunteered to book the band when it had never even played a show outside of Southern California. In those early days, Rick and Jean would spend hours arranging shows and short minitours for blink that often earned the band only twenty-five dollars. Because the Bondes were paid a percentage of what the band made, Rick and Jean would receive less than five dollars for hours of hard work. Their generosity gave blink a chance to be seen and heard outside of their hometown. Rick and Jean Bonde would continue to work with blink until 2000, when the Tahoe Agency officially retired. Their years of service had an irreplaceable affect on blink's lives and career.

Unfortunately, the success of *Cheshire Cat* didn't only draw good attention. It also caught the eye of the other Blink, an Irish techno band that the San Diego blink had not known existed. The Irish Blink took exception to sharing their name and filed a cease-and-desist order requiring the punk band to stop using the name "Blink." Unwilling to engage in a legal battle, the San Diego band complied with the order; however, they would not give up the name "Blink" entirely. They had worked too hard to make the name "Blink" recognizable to just walk away from it completely. To differentiate themselves from the Irish Blink, the San Diego band simply added a number to the end of their name. The number 182 was chosen completely at random. Mark and Tom might try to convince you otherwise, but they are dirty liars. Blink-182 was born.

The Capers Of Rick DeVoe, Part One

In 1997, blink-182 was on tour in Florida. Friend and manager Rick DeVoe came to help the band out on a couple of shows. On one particular night, Rick took the night off, relaxed, and had some beers with the boys. And as they always do when Rick drinks, things turned interesting.

The club blink-182 was playing in was located next door to a male strip club. In fact, there was a door connecting the two establishments. The strip club was packed with screaming, hooting, dancing women ogling the nearly naked men on stage. The action next door was almost better than the crowd at the punk club at which blink-182 was playing.

The guys had stuck their heads through the connecting door to laugh at the strip-club antics when, before they knew what was going on, Rick rushed up onto the stage, pushed the featured male performer off, and began to strip for the scores of screaming women. Rick threw his pants to one woman, his shirt to another, all of whom ate it up. The place went wild.

But it was the bouncers that grabbed the naked Rick, tackling him and dragging him from the stage.

The blink-182 guys were laughing so hard they couldn't do a thing to help their manager. And their laughter only got worse when Rick started explaining to the bouncers that it was okay, they didn't have to call the police, he wasn't crazy. He was just the manager of the band performing next door.

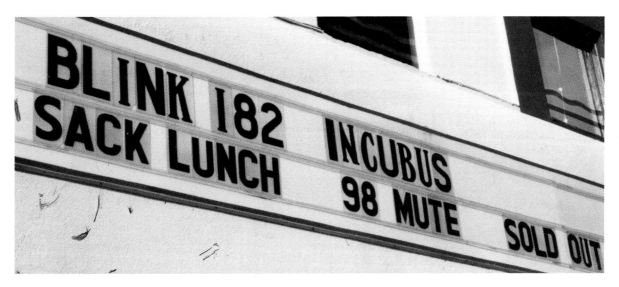

"I'm a ninja of the masturbatory arts."
—Tom Delonge

5 America was so innocent then, so bliss-
fully unaware of what was about to be
unleashed on their sons and daughters.
Blink-182 was loose, and they were
coming to a town near you.

It was 1995 and blink-182 was ready to hit
the road, to reach outside their home base of
Southern California. They were ready, but
leaving town was a lot easier said than done.

Logistically, these out-of-town shows were
hard. Blink-182 did not have the resources to
buy a van or any other mode of transportation that would carry all three musicians and
their equipment. At first, Mark, Tom, and
Scott would each drive their own separate
cars to shows, every inch filled with equipment, leaving just enough room for the driver.
But no one wanted to do this for any show

that required large amounts of driving. And
buying a van simply wasn't smart until the
band had been offered a real tour that would
justify the expense.

But blink-182 wasn't about to let something
silly like having no transportation stop them
from playing these far-away places. They
would do whatever they had to do to reach
new audiences. Their options? Borrow or
rent. Neither of which worked out so well.

For example, Tom and Mark borrowed a van
from good friends Unwritten Law to play a
show in Reno, Nevada. The Unwritten Law
van was an old, tan, hollowed-out deathtrap
commonly referred to as "The Cock." (The
van earned the nickname following a show in
Salt Lake City when UL drew a huge wiener
in the dust on the side of the van to catch the

41

42 eye of the notoriously conservative city.) The van had only a driver's seat and passenger seat, leaving the rest of the van for cargo space. It had no heat and no air conditioning. But it moved.

Mark, Tom, and I (who was pulling T-shirt duty at the time), were the unlucky three that made this trip. Scott was already in Reno where he was living at the time. Lucky bastard.

The ride was extremely crowded with the band's equipment filling almost every inch of the van. Only by pushing the two front seats all the way forward, was a tiny space cleared for a third passenger. It was not a comfortable place to sit, either. Besides the cramped position one had to assume just to fit, there was also the bigger concern of the Teetering

Amps of Death. At every turn or stop, the equipment shifted, coming dangerously close to toppling over onto the poor third passenger, me.

To make the ride even more pleasurable was the frigid winter weather. The mountains were deep with snow that glistened in the silver moonlight—but Mark, Tom, and I didn't give a crap about silver moonlight, because it was below freezing and The Cock had no damn heat. It was absolutely arctic and the Southern Californians hadn't really come prepared.

Tom: "God, that drive sucked. It was awful. But, you know, we had a show. None of that mattered because it was way too important to us to play a show, especially outside of San Diego."

Finally, The Cock pulled into Reno, and the three of them were rewarded with an incredible show. Blink-182 played that night with Face to Face at a tiny club called the Fallout Shelter. Face to Face was one of blink-182's favorite bands, and they were stoked to play with them. Not to mention, the kids totally went off for blink-182 and the awful drive was all but forgotten.

Until they tried to leave, that is, and The Cock wouldn't start. Wouldn't even turn over. Nothing. A roadie for Face to Face noticed their troubles and came to the trio's rescue. He rigged the van to start, but warned that if the van was turned off it would never start again. So, the drive home ended up no better than the drive to Reno. Tom, Mark, and I drove for twelve hours straight—stopping for food, getting gas, braving the cold once

more—without turning off the ignition. The drive was marked by constant praying that The Cock wouldn't do anything stupid, like die completely or blow up. That was the end of the borrowing days.

Mark: "That was scary. We had to fill up with the van running. I was just waiting for that thing to explode."

Rental vans were mechanically better, but posed their own problems. Mark was the only one in the band of legal age to drive a rental. On one breakneck jaunt through California and down to Las Vegas and Phoenix, Mark drove every mile of the trip, going for nearly a week without sleeping more than a few hours. Tom and Scott were quite well rested, **43** though, and generally enjoyed the entire experience.

44 Mark: "It sucked. I didn't sleep for like five days or something. It just killed me. There was no way I could keep doing that."

Just when blink had run out of other transportation options, they found their justification for buying a van. They were blessed with the tour they had been waiting for. Taylor Steele, the best damn surf-video producer in the world, and good friend of manager Rick DeVoe, had an offer for blink-182. In the fall of 1995 he was releasing a new surf video called *GoodTimes,* and he planned a national tour to premiere the video featuring bands from the soundtrack.

And so, blink-182 purchased their one and only tour van, a white Chevy Beauville they christened "The Millennium Falcon," in honor of *Star Wars.* Cargo Records had to cosign for the loan, but the van was all blink-182's. The Falcon was to take the boys of blink-182 on many an adventure.

The first being the GoodTimes Tour which began in October of 1995. Not quite knowing what to expect, blink-182 loaded their equipment into a trailer and threw their suitcases in the back of The Falcon and headed out. As a road crew and for moral support, the band brought along Mike "Cuban Missile Crisis" Lucena, "Castro" for short, and Cam "Vegan" Jones.

The tour started in California, headed across the southwest, into the southern states, including Florida, and up the Eastern Seaboard, ending in New Jersey. GoodTimes featured blink-182, Unwritten Law, Sprung Monkey, and punk legends Seven Seconds.

All the bands were awesome friends, and the shows were great from the start. How could they not be great with such an incredible lineup? Blink's first tour could not possibly have been better.

Mark: "The GoodTimes tour was awesome. It was our first tour, and we were playing with such great bands. I mean, we were a nothing little band playing with punk-rock legends. Every night I was stoked just to watch them play. And that they were all cool guys and my friends, that was a huge bonus."

Tom: "Our first tour was super cool. It was our first time out, so everything was new and exciting. Even the drives seemed shorter on that tour. Plus, we got to tour with bands I listened to all the time, bands I dreamed about playing with."

Besides playing with such great bands, blink-182 would get in more trouble and have more fun in the thirty days of GoodTimes than they ever thought humanly possible.

The daily drives from town to town were filled with Castro's Scarface impressions and dangerous high-speed highway maneuverings to get into the perfect position to moon the other bands' vans. Cam played terrible music that no one else liked, but came up with such hilarious defenses that he was allowed to listen to it anyway. At least when the rest of the van's occupants were sleeping. The band had a habit of playing the lottery, and losing,

in every state they passed through, decorating the inside of the van with the scratched off stubs. The back of the van was plastered over with stickers purchased at truck stops with slogans like "I Brake for Boys." (The stickers eventually were removed when the band noticed they were being pulled over much too often.) The band was adapting quickly to life on the road. They learned to create their fun if they couldn't find it.

In Dallas, blink-182 spent the afternoon exploring historic Dealy Plaza where President Kennedy was assassinated. (Tom swears the assassination occurred because Kennedy had learned about the aliens living under Florida.)

Later that night, at the Dallas club The Engine Room, the band began their own lives of crime. No one remembers who first saw the life-size cardboard cutout of Lenny Kravitz, but the entire blink-182 team instantly knew they had to have it. Problem was, it belonged to the promoter, and it was standing in his office.

Mark: "After we played our set, we loaded up our equipment, got in the van, turned on the engine, and sent Castro running back into the club to grab Lenny. It was so funny. Castro kidnapped a stupid cardboard Lenny Kravitz thing. He came running out to the van, carrying Lenny, with bouncers chasing after him. As soon as he jumped in, we just took off. I don't even know what happened to that thing."

46　Always looking to incorporate some education into their lives, blink-182 watched a rocket get launched into outer space from Cape Canaveral in Florida. "Dude, I thought that would be really lame, but it was actually pretty gnarly," Mark admits.

And Tom, taking the lives-of-crime joke too far, got himself arrested. On Halloween night, at the Milkbar in Jacksonville, Tom made a major mistake. Despite being warned that the Jacksonville police were cracking down on Halloween "crime," Tom, who was underage at the time, drank quite a bit. Which might still have been okay, if he hadn't wandered out into the streets still firmly grasping his bottle of beer. The cops were on him in seconds. When Tom failed to provide proof of age, they called for a car, and Tom was handcuffed and thrown in the back seat. Ironically, he was wearing a Down By Law T-shirt at the time.

Tom: "The funny thing is, when I was arrested I didn't think it was anything bad. The cop came over to me and right away said, 'Somebody's going to jail.' And I was like, 'I wonder who.' Even when they put me in handcuffs I was pretty sure something was going to work out. They put me in the car, I was still okay. But then, when the police car was driving away, and I looked back and saw all of my friends waving bye-bye, that's when I was like 'Hey, wait, this is really bad!'"

Tom spent that night in jail, and might have stayed longer. However, Rick DeVoe was able to make arrangements to post bail and plead Tom guilty to the misdemeanor, ending the whole fiasco before the tour had moved on minus one act.

Tom: "The night I spent in jail sucked. First, they strip searched me and put me in convict clothes. Then they stuck me in this room with like forty big, scary, criminal guys. I had to go to the bathroom so bad, and there was only one toilet in the middle of the room and no toilet paper because the big, scary men were using the rolls for pillows. Then, they moved me into a smaller room where it was just me and this guy named Roger. Roger kept telling me he was going to eat my grits. I didn't even know what grits were! Man, that sucked so bad."

Luckily, Tom's stay in jail was limited to that one awful night, and the band continued on with the tour.

The next band adventure was an all-out bar fight. At a show in South Carolina the bands took exception to the amount of force the bouncers were using with the kids. Words were exchanged, some comments made about mothers' sexual habits and certain people's attractions to dogs, and the next thing anyone knew, it was the Old West—punches were flying, chairs were thrown, and bottles were breaking.

Mark: "It was gnarly. It was like Road House or something. Our roadie Castro actually had a barstool smashed across his back. He got big punk credibility points for that."

Then there were the on-going Roman candle wars.

Tom: "Somehow, we just kept getting more and more fireworks every day. We had a big war going between us and Unwritten Law. But it was really every man for himself.

GOOD·TIMES
A TAYLOR STEELE VIDEO
TOUR & VIDEO PREMIER

PENNYWISE

blink-182

P-wt

THE LAST TWO SHOWS OF THE TOU

JAN.26 & JAN.2
* FRIDAY *   * SATUDAY *

MR.CROWNS • SOMA

We'd shoot Roman candles at each other's vans on the freeway; we'd shot at each other in parking lots, on the beaches. It was fun."

But it wasn't long before the vicious fighting claimed an innocent victim. It was late at night on a deserted Atlantic beach. A Roman candle fired at Castro landed in the hood of his sweatshirt and began to smolder. Of course, Castro couldn't see behind his own head and apparently didn't smell the smoke, because he wouldn't believe any one's yells that he was on fire. "Ha ha, you guys! I'm not going to fall for that trick!" he kept yelling as he ran farther and farther away from his former enemies who were now trying to help him. Eventually, he realized that it had not been a ruse to get him to let his guard down. He was actually on fire. Castro wasn't hurt, but the sweatshirt was ruined. Oh well, it wasn't Castro's anyway. He had borrowed it from the other roadie, Cam. Cam is the innocent victim referred to. Castro got exactly what he deserved.

And in between all the hijinks and well, good times, blink actually played shows! In fact, they played a lot of shows to a lot of kids. And the kids were loving it. Touring with such great bands was giving blink more and more |exposure. Kids were buying *Cheshire Cat* and passing it on to their friends. (We know who you are, and you will be sued for copyright infringement.) Blink-182 was definitely catching on. The tour made a huge difference and for the first time, the guys could imagine kids all across America listening to their music.

The boys were excited about their newly budding musical careers, but they were also ready to head home. Unfortunately, in order to get there, blink-182 had to drive seventy-two straight hours from New Jersey to San Diego and catch a flight to Hawaii for the tour's last show. Not that Hawaii wasn't worth it.

The boys had completed their first tour. The experience had been an education.

Mark: "Tour is fun, but it's hard work, too. When you dream about it, you never think it's going to be hard. You're either doing nothing, sitting in the van bored as fuck, or you're running around like crazy trying to get shit done. Or you're on stage, which is always the best part."

Tom: "Before we did our first tour, I thought there was less sitting for hours involved in tour. But who cares, it's still fun."

Life on the road could be pretty tough on a guy. Especially on those early tours.

Imagine. You are away from home for months. You spend most of your days sitting in a van. And a lot of your nights, too. If you're not sitting in the van, you're sitting in a club. And all the clubs are exactly the same. Instead of sleeping in your own warm bed, you are sleeping in the van, or sleeping on the floor at someone's house, or if you are lucky, sharing a hotel room with five other people. As for pooping in dirty club bathrooms everyday, here's a tip: Use the girls'

50 bathroom. It's usually cleaner and always has toilet paper. You might want to have someone stand guard for you, though. Any money made goes directly back into the gas fund. You only have five dollars and it has to feed you all day. You eat nothing but crappy fast food, or on a good night, Denny's.

Mark: "In all those early tours, I just remember going to bed hungry. We'd wait until after the show to get dinner, and then it'd be super late and we could never find any place to eat."

You do the same thing every single day, but you're always in a new place. The change of scenery does little to alleviate the boredom. In fact, after a while you don't even notice the changes.

The Capers Of Rick DeVoe, Part Two
The Lex Luthor Years

In 1996, in the midst of the Shitty Weather Tour, Rick DeVoe joined blink-182 for their first international show. The band was playing Quebec, Canada. The show was a huge success, and to celebrate, Rick had a couple of beers. Actually, he had a lot of couple of beers.

At the end of the night, Rick headed towards the merch table to see if kids were buying blink-182 CDs and T-shirts. Many of them were, but Rick was frustrated at those who weren't. As a bizarre alchohol-induced sales tactic, Rick climbed on top of the table and started shouting at the departing kids.

"I am Lex Luthor, I am strong," he yelled, though only Rick knows why.

When the kids seemed frightened and confused by Rick's behavior, he thought perhaps it was the language barrier. After all, these kids were mostly French speakers. So, in an effort to communicate, he tried another language, Spanish, which they don't speak in Quebec. The poor kids had no idea what the tall, skinny American was yelling at them. Frightened, all they could do was flee.

You lose all perspective on tour; it is all routine—drive, wait, play, sleep, drive, wait, play, and on and on and on. It also completely lacks the sort of structure that the rest of the world operates on; time becomes measured primarily in the length of the drives. The concept of days of the week and actual dates is pretty much lost on tour, so is physical location. Ask any band on the road where they are, or what day it is, and you'll most likely get an I-don't-know for an answer.

Because you are living in such close quarters with the same people day in and day out, the smallest habits become huge annoyances. You will spend at least a few days hating your band's guts. But whatever the annoy-ances, tour isn't all bad. Touring is superfun, too. Because you got to do cool crap like have Roman candle wars, and the people

who were there with you were your true friends who went through hell to help you out. You spend a lot of time laughing on these tours, even if nothing is funny.

Scott: "There were plenty of times I laughed until I cried."

Unfortunately, once you do your first tour, you develop a taste for it. And as stoked as the guys were to be back in San Diego, after about a week, blink got antsy. They were ready for their next tour.

Their next tour was actually the same tour, but on a different continent. The GoodTimes tour, with Pennywise joining on to headline, headed to Australia, where people talk funny and yell things like "Go off!" and "Filth!" In Australia, the kids are far, far crazier, and the beer has way more alcohol in it.

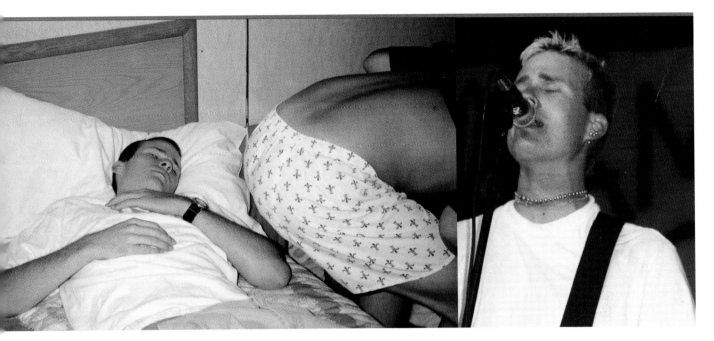

Blink almost didn't make it to Oz. For a new band with little money, the plane tickets were prohibitively expensive. Until punk-rock superstars Pennywise stepped in to save the day. Pennywise has always stood by young start-up bands. An awesome band made up of awesome people, Pennywise paid for all of blink's plane tickets, making it possible for the beginners to introduce themselves to the land Down Under.

That's not the only way Pennywise gave blink a generous hand up. While punk was an established movement in other places in the world, it was just starting to take off in Australia. Green Day wasn't even big in Australia. But Pennywise was the forerunner for punk Down Under. They were huge. To be able to play with Pennywise every night put blink on the top of the list with the Oz

punkers. Blink could not believe the crowd reaction they got down there. The Australians were receptive to blink-182 right from the start. Australia is still one of blink's favorite places to play.

After their brief tour overseas, blink had only a short time off before they headed back out onto America's highways. Though it had seemed to take forever to get that first tour, now that they had been initiated into the world of life on the road, blink entered a period of almost nonstop touring, finishing out 1995 on the road.

In 1996 blink began playing with Pennywise and Unwritten Law in Alaska for the King of the Hill snowboarding competition. Alaska was awesome. All three members of blink had grown up in the surf-skate-snow community, and the guys were excited to have the opportunity to snowboard in Alaska, which they were pretty sure had better snow than Southern California. They hitchhiked out to a mountain where they spent the afternoon riding a helicopter to the top and then attempting to stand up on their boards all the way to the bottom. Mark is pretty sure that in one vicious fall, he actually ripped his butt in two. He never went back to claim the half he left behind on that snowy peak.

Later that night, Tom made the unwise decision to play a little practical joke on Fletcher from Pennywise.

Tom: "I'd heard all these stories about Fletcher, about how gnarly his tricks were. But I thought they were all talk. So, Scott and I planned to break into his room and dump a bucket of snow on him. I thought it would be funny, and I didn't think he'd do anything too gnarly back. I was standing outside Pennywise's door with the bucket of snow when the door opened and I got hit with a bunch of water. They caught me before I could do anything. I thought that was the end of it."

Tom was wrong. It was far from the end of it.

That night, Mark, Tom, and Scott decided to err on the side of caution as they went to bed. They locked the door, bolted it, put the chain on, and for good measure wedged a heavy guitar case under the doorknob. In the middle of the night, Tom felt a tap on his shoulder. It was Mark. He woke Tom and pointed at the door.

Tom: "I looked at the door and you could see the door buckling. 'Cause there was a huge six-foot, six-inch, three-hundred-pound guy on the other side of it trying to knock it down."

And then the door opened.

Mark: "What really sucked about the whole thing is that the door almost held. Fletcher gave up for a second 'cause the door wasn't giving. Then he gave it one more push and the damn thing opened. I did what any man would do. I ran outside in my underwear."

Tom ran into the bathroom and, despite the three guys trying to stop him, managed to lock the door behind him. That left poor Scott, who was still sleeping, unaware of the break-in, to take the brunt of the revenge. Scott, finally awake and very confused, was herded into the corner of the room where he was doused with Mylanta, "shot" with squirt guns filled with hot sauce, and shocked with a contraption Fletcher had devised from a car battery. As a finale, Pennywise threw all of blink's belongings out the hotel window into the snow.

Tom: "Our manager Rick was in the room right below us. It was the middle of the night and he started hearing people running back and forth in our room. Then he looked out his window and just saw suitcases and clothes flying by. He knew we'd been hit."

After the invaders left, Tom and Scott waited for things to quiet down before they

wandered into the hall. They learned then that Unwritten Law had also been molested that night. Pennywise had set off multiple fire extinguishers in UL's room, covering everything in white powder.

Tom: "As hotel security and the local police arrived, there were five dudes with their asses completely kicked standing in the hallway in just their boxers."

The bands were allowed to stay at the hotel for the rest of that night, but were not welcome any longer. Which was fine with them. They were all flying home the next day.

After Alaska, blink-182 headed back out on tour in February 1996, playing two final weeks with the GoodTimes tour on the West Coast. Then, they immediately headed off on their first headlining tour across America.

They called this tour the Shitty Weather tour.

Now accustomed to the road, blink-182 knew what to expect. They thought this tour would be easy, but it actually ended up being one of the most "punk" punk-rock tours they would ever do. This was only blink-182's second U.S. tour, and they were now the main band on the bill. If kids were going to come to the show, they were going to do it solely on blink-182's draw. While blink-182 had already become popular in some parts of the country, other parts were still holding out. There were shows where only thirty kids came. The van was especially crowded that tour, with the three band members: Cam pulling guitar tech duty, I was in charge of the money and the merchandise, and tour newcomer Mike Fasold was the jack-of-all-trades. There was not enough room to get comfortable in the van, and the drives on this tour were particularly long. With the close quarters, there was no way to avoid anyone's germs, and sicknesses were passed back and forth for the entire tour, including a terrifying pink-eye scare that ended up being only psychosomatic.

And, of course, as the name might suggest, the weather was awful. Beginning on their second day out, the Southern Californians hit snow, and stayed in it for half the tour. A particular low point was in Chicago where blink-182 played with a band that dressed entirely in white jumpsuits and tried to coordinate their movements with pre-recorded video sequences.

Mark: "Our dressing rooms were connected. I asked them if they needed any help

The Capers Of Rick DeVoe, Part Three

On the band's last night in Australia, they made plans to meet with reps from Mushroom Records, the Australian distributor for *Cheshire Cat*. Rick DeVoe had spent much of that afternoon drinking and when dinner rolled around he was not in good shape. When the car with blink, Rick, and the reps pulled into a lot next to a glass building, Rick jumped out of the car, pulled off all of his clothes, and started dancing for the people he could see sitting on the other side of the glass. While Rick was busy shaking his stuff, blink-182 and the record-label reps filed into the building. The glass building was a restaurant, in fact, it was the restaurant where the group was having dinner. Rick turned around just in time to see his friends laugh at him as they walked through the door. It was pretty damn funny.

But it didn't end there. Rick proceeded to make a scene inside the restaurant as well. He defined "loud American" and eventually tried to start a food fight. The evening was closed out with Jim from Pennywise peeing under the dinner table. That wasn't quite as funny. The label reps weren't terribly amused by any of it. Luckily, that was the band's last night in Australia. They left just in time to miss the newspaper headlines decrying the rude behavior of a group of obnoxious Americans in a posh Australian restaurant.

changing out of those white jumpsuits, but they weren't into it. In fact, they slammed the door in my face."

The entire blink-182 crew was sick. The roads were either deep in snow or coated with ice, preventing most kids from making their way out to the show, so only a handful of people watched the set. The venue was almost as cold inside as it was outside, and in the merch area, wind was blowing the snow inside through huge cracks in the wall.

Anne: "It was just way too cold. I walked out to the van in the morning after I had just gotten out of the shower. My hair was still wet, and in just five minutes, my braids were frozen solid. Then, I got to the venue and they wanted me to sell T-shirts in what was basically a snow-drift. No way. I refused to do it."

It wasn't a good night.

To make matters worse, the band had to leave as soon as the show was over to make a seventeen-hour drive to Quebec City in Canada for their next show.

Of course, the drive wouldn't have been seventeen hours long if it hadn't been for the biggest snowstorm to hit the Northeast in forty years. The snow was falling so fast and so heavy that it was nearly impossible to see the road at all. Tom, who had previously driven huge trucks at his job delivering cement, was elected the most qualified driver, despite the fact that he had failed his drivers' test multiple times. He would drive all seventeen hours.

Tom: "It was scary. I didn't know anything about driving in the snow, but I just trusted

58 myself more to do it. I just kept driving and driving and driving. You couldn't even see anything it was snowing so hard. And we'd hit ice, and the whole van would just slide. It was gnarly."

No one slept that entire drive. No one even relaxed. Everyone sat bolt upright in their seats, seat belts securely fastened, hands and feet inside the vehicle for all seventeen hours. The conditions were so bad blink-182 began to think they should just get off the road. But if they stopped, they would never make the show. They reasoned with themselves that the best drivers in the world are truckers. If the truckers are still driving, then the roads are still driveable. There were still trucks, so blink-182 kept going. When they stopped seeing truckers on the road, they were in the middle of nowhere and half way there. This

time they didn't even bother reasoning. They just kept going. When the band finally emerged from the storm, it was at the border checkpoint to enter Canada where they had to wait for hours for their Canadian work permits to be issued and for their van to be searched before they would cross into Canada where their hotel rooms waited. They were exhausted and hungry. The standard hassle at the border didn't help lighten their moods. They were not happy. To add insult to injury, the only other vehicle they had seen on the road in that awful storm had been a police car. A police car that immediately pulled them over and gave them a ticket for driving *under* the speed limit. But, they made their show.

Mark: "At one point, we stopped and called Rick who was meeting us in Canada. We didn't know if we were going to be able to

keep driving. Rick just kept telling us, 'Dude, it's not that bad, you just gotta keep going. Don't puss out.' Then, after this shitty super-scary drive, we get to Canada and Rick is sitting backstage drinking hot chocolate, all warm and happy and shit. We all wanted to kick his ass."

The show made it all worthwhile. It was SnoJam, a popular festival show in Canada, and the lineup was filled with big names from the punk world, including Bouncing Souls, Ten Foot Pole, No Use For A Name, and 88 Fingers Louie. Though blink-182 had never played in Canada before, and the kids in the audience spoke mostly French, and Mark was wearing a pink, fake-leather women's belt, the crowd could not get enough of the three San Diego punks. Within an hour of the doors opening, I sold out of

merchandise at the T-shirt table. Tired of repeating, "*Je n'ai pas plus,*" which I really hopes means "I don't have anymore," I abandoned the table. I hated that kids would leave the show with nothing, and began to make rounds through the venue handing out stickers. This turned out to be a dangerous operation. I would hand out two or three before I would be surrounded by a mob of kids, reaching and grabbing until I couldn't take it anymore. I would throw the stickers in the air and run for my life, letting the kids fight it out. But those kids got their stickers, and they'd better appreciate it, dammit.

Besides being an incredible show, the festival treated the bands well, offering blink their first comfortable night's sleep since the tour had begun. The SnoJam tour set each band up in a small condo at the local ski resort and gave them free passes for the day. They also gave every member of every band the same red snowboarding jacket, which made it painfully obvious the following day on the slopes who was with the tour and who wasn't. The lodge was filled with an army of punks in bright red jackets. It was a sight to see.

After Canada, blink-182 and the snow headed down the eastern seaboard into the southern states. Along the way the band would hit torrential flooding rains, tornado warnings, and a record-breaking heat wave. It was the Shitty Weather tour. Finally, they crossed the Southwest and made it home to San Diego.

Band Pranks

Blink-182 has a well-earned reputation for making life difficult for those who work with them, especially professional people like managers and tour managers and record execs.

Some famous pranks have included:

• Using an MCA rep's e-mail account to send a companywide e-mail informing all employees of MCA that the sender of the e-mail would like to come out of the closet.

• Adding sexual lines to postcards sent to promoters and others in the music industry by Rick DeVoe.

• Changing one tour manager's outgoing message on his answering machine to include the line, "I love men. Call me."

• Sabotaging tour managers' laptops and programming the computers to spew sexual language while booting up. Usually, when a tour manager boots up his computer he is in a room full of promoters and other important people.

Wasting Time – 1996 Australian Tour EP

"Vegetables. A waste of good plate space."

—*Twist* Magazine, August 2000

6 Cargo Records had signed blink before anyone knew who blink was. They had opened doors for the band, helped them buy their tour van, go on tour, and had made it possible for the kids of America to buy the band's first CD, *Cheshire Cat.* But Cargo Records was not perfect, and problems were starting to become apparent in the relationship between band and label.

Blink-182 will never regret their initial decision to sign with the San Diego label. But by the end of 1995 they also had no doubt that it was time to move on. Eric Goodis, president of Cargo, had always stood behind blink-182, and there were others in the office that supported the trio as well, but the majority of the staff at the label still looked upon blink as potty-mouthed kids, not as musicians.

Mark: "I wouldn't change our decision to go with Cargo, but there were only three or four people there that believed in us at all. This guy Jeff, Larry Monroe, Eric Goodis, and Laura. And O would always try to get people behind us, but most of the people there didn't like our band. They would work for us, but only because it was their jobs, not because they liked our band. They didn't like that Southern California punk-rock stuff."

These people often overlooked blink-182 and chose to work with the other bands on the label, bands who seemed to take themselves more seriously.

In reality, blink-182 took their careers as musicians very seriously. It was the music that had first inspired Mark, Tom, and Scott, prompted them to start a band, and from day

GRILLED CHEESE   BLINK-182 GRL 703

BLINK-182
"LEMMINGS"

THE JOURNAL OF THE NATIONAL GYNECOLOGY SOCIETY SAN DIEGO, CA

blink-182
THEY CAME TO CONQUER...

URANUS

62 one they had given it their all. The band was touring nonstop to introduce blink-182 to every part of the country. They were distraught when they began to hear more and more kids complain that they could not find *Cheshire Cat* in any of their local record stores. Attempts to order the CD were futile as well. The album simply wasn't reaching the fans.

Cheshire Cat was two years old, and it was time for blink-182 to record a new album. In the interim they had released two seven-inch recordings with Cargo, *They Came to Conquer Uranus* and *Lemmings,* both featuring new songs the guys had written in the years since *Cheshire Cat.* But the band had a wealth of new material, and interest in the band was high. Now was the time to hit the audience with a new CD.

Blink-182 was concerned, however, with releasing the new CD with Cargo Records. They were worried that the label's lack of distribution would hinder kids' ability to find the album, like it did with *Cheshire Cat.* Different record labels were courting the band, and blink-182 began to seriously consider moving on.

Choosing a label is one of the most frightening and most difficult decisions to make.

Mark: "Choosing a label is like getting married after only one date."

Most important to blink-182 was keeping control of their band. They had created the band, and they knew where they wanted to take their creation. They didn't want anyone else to decide their fate. They wanted complete artistic control and the power to say no

to anything they felt was wrong for the band. The band also wanted a label that had the ability to place their CD in every record store in America. They wanted a fan in the middle of Iowa to be able to buy a blink-182 CD as easily as a fan in L.A. They also wanted a label that would stand behind them, that would support them and do everything they could to help blink-182 build a career in music. After all, the guys were getting pretty sick of living with their parents.

Beginning in March 1996, several labels courted the band, sending A&R reps to shows, and inviting the band to stop by the office for lunch meetings. Among those interested were Epic, Atlantic, Interscope, Columbia, and MCA. And major labels weren't the only ones that came calling. Influential indie labels were also looking to bring blink on board, including

Epitaph Records, a label that carried such punk greats as close friends Pennywise and punk giants Bad Religion.

With so much to consider, blink-182 spent the spring and summer of 1996 contemplating their options. Several times they thought they had reached a final decision.

Tom: "Tom Whalley, the big guy at Interscope, stuck with us for like six months. He was supercool. One time he came out to a show in Las Vegas, and the vulgarity on stage got really gnarly—dog semen and horrible stuff. I saw the look on his face, and I thought that if he made it through that night we were going to have to sign with his label."

Tom Whalley did make it through the night, but the guys still weren't sure. Blink-182 also took a serious look at Epitaph, trusting

64 in the label's ability to work in the punk world. But it was a revisit to a label they had previously written off that would decide the label issue for blink-182.

When MCA first made an offer, the guys hadn't given it too much thought. The label was riding out a dead spell, and was derisively referred to in the music industry as MCA—Musicians' Cemetery of America. But MCA wouldn't give up, and their persistence, and obvious sincerity began to win over Mark, Tom, and Scott.

Tom: "MCA was buying Cargo, and they really wanted us, too. They said they wanted us to be their success story. They had a whole new team of people, and they wanted to sign something new and good. Us."

MCA understood blink's requests and guaranteed the musicians complete artistic control. The label wasn't interested in changing the band. They were interested in taking the band as what they were, and doing their best to help the band succeed. Blink found the staff at the label were honest, straightforward people in touch with the music world, rather than stuffy businessmen who placed more emphasis on the bottom line. The more blink-182 talked to these people, the more they liked them.

When a final offer was put on the table, blink-182 signed it. After months of deliberation, they were confident they were making the right decision. MCA had incredible distribution. It was an honest label with honest people who would not leave the band on a back burner. They would allow

blink-182 to remain true to themselves, giving the band ultimate control. This was, without a doubt, the best decision for the band.

Time would prove that they did make the right decision. MCA would help to bring blink-182 further then they had ever dreamed possible.

MCA Rep Darren Wolf: "The guys have worked so hard for us. As a label we really respect what they do for their band. When we signed blink-182, they ran themselves. They toured and had merchandise. They had already built their own fan base. They didn't really need us. They make it so easy as a label. They are so smart; they really know their audience. They did all the dirty work. We just took what they already were and

made it bigger. They had the groundswell, we just turned it into a wave. . . . They're music nerds, we're label nerds, and all nerds get along."

MCA did keep their promise of awarding artistic control to the band. However, MCA did have to step in on two occasions, once when blink-182 wanted to feature a spoof of the Macarena on *Dude Ranch* called "Hey Wipe Your Anus," and again when blink suggested recording a song for *Enema of the State* called "I Want to Fuck a Dog in the Ass." Blink-182 will now humbly concede that MCA was right on both counts. Those songs weren't such good ideas. Even for blink-182.

The Original "Josie" Video

Few fans know that the familiar "Josie" video, featuring Alyssa Milano, is actually the second video blink-182 shot for the song.

Originally, the band attempted to film a video with a more "serious" look. They turned to a new director. Not only was it the band's first time working with the director, it was the director's first video ever.

In this video, the band was to be practicing in a basement. One of the musicians accidentally hits a pipe with his guitar causing a significant leak. The basement fills with water, but the band plays on. Ultimately, the band is completely underwater.

Though the band had some hesitations regarding the premise, they were willing to give it a shot. Almost immediately they regretted their decision.

"Filming the first 'Josie' video was awful. We had to spend hours submerged in water, swimming around in this tank thing. We had to bring old equipment that we were willing to ruin. It was no fun," Mark remembers.

Tom agrees, "All I remember about filming that video was that it was freezing cold. It was like forty degrees and we either had to be underwater, or sprayed down with water. I cut my head open on shrapnel that was floating around in the water. It sucked."

After all of that, the band didn't even like the resulting video. They were unhappy with the look of the video and didn't feel it worked for the song.

"After all we went through, it didn't even look cool. It just looked like we were playing in some water or something," Tom comments.

Unwilling to release the video as it was, blink-182 scrapped the project completely. They turned instead to director Darren Doane who had filmed their two earlier videos.

"We knew Darren could do something funny for us. We liked what he had done with 'M&Ms' and 'Dammit,' so we trusted he could do something good with this. And we were stoked with how 'Josie' turned out. It's awesome," Mark adds.

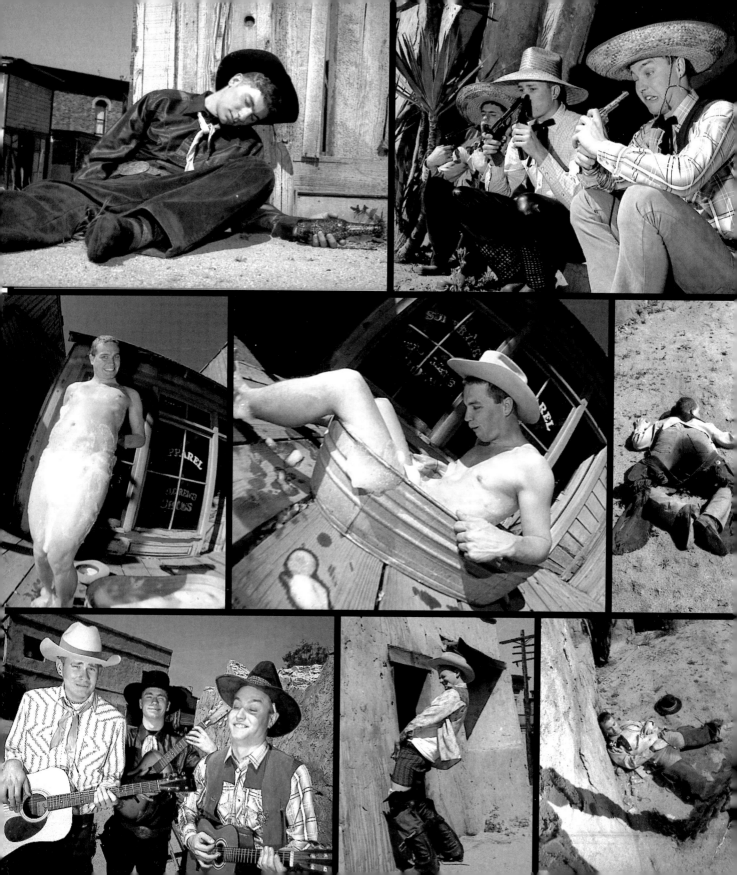

—Mark Hoppus conjugating fellatio as a verb for "We all get blow jobs."

"Fellatamos."
—*Smug* **Magazine, Feb/March 2000**

7 When blink-182 entered the studio in late 1996, they were as giddy as schoolgirls. Although the band had previously recorded two demo cassettes and one full-length CD, they had still only spent less than one week in the studio. This time around the band had the time and money to record the album they had always wanted.

Dude Ranch was recorded over the period of a month at Big Fish Studios in Rancho Santa Fe, California during a gray, gloomy winter. The studio is actually a converted guesthouse on a large piece of property in a swank area of San Diego.

Mark: "The whole recording of *Dude Ranch* feels cloudy to me. That's how the weather was everyday. It was cloudy all the time. So that's what I think of."

The drive to the studio was on a narrow twisting road that alternately passed through wooded areas and horse farms. (Mark would like to warn everyone that cops tend to hang out here—he got a speeding ticket on the way to the studio.) Unfortunately, the area was still recovering from destructive wildfires that had torn through the countryside just a few months earlier. The black, charred path of the fire passed only a few feet behind Big Fish, and the studio had come within inches of being burned to the ground. Of course, what was surely a tragedy to homeowners in the area was merely fodder for Mark and Tom's jokes. When taking breaks from recording, the two would often use the depressing burn areas as the backdrop to the "movies" they were always filming with Mark's new video camera. An example of their excellent filmmaking skills behind Big Fish Studios can be seen at the beginning of blink-182's "Urethra Chronicles" video where Tom is a nature film narrator and Mark plays the nature, running through the burnt landscape in just his boxers and repeatedly spanking himself. Tragically, the Oscar committee shunned it.

But between takes on the "movie set" blink-182 had other things to do at the studio, like playing mah-jongg on the computer and reading the articles from the shelves and shelves of *Playboy*s that the studio had thoughtfully provided.

Mark: "Seriously, that guy had every single copy of *Playboy* from like 1955 on. It was gnarly."

There was also lunch to eat, almost always brought from Sombrero, and dinner, usually Chinese food from Pick Up Stix in Encinitas.

Incidentally, there was also an album to record. This second album blink-182 was determined to make sound as good as humanly possible, especially since they had waited almost two years since *Cheshire Cat*.

Before heading to Big Fish, Mark, Tom, and Scott booked time at DML Studios in Escondido, California, where they perfected the songs for *Dude Ranch*. The songs had been written periodically over the last year in

the living room of Tom's mom's house, in the warehouse where Tom worked, and in other such random places.

Tom: "I remember writing most of those songs in my living room, sitting on a curb, whatever. But I can totally remember writing those songs. Back then, each song was pretty much written with a specific girl or event in mind."

Mark and Tom were both excited about making a new album, and songs just kept coming. Tom was infamous in those days for bringing an acoustic guitar almost everywhere with him.

Mark was experiencing the same creative surge. The guitar line for "Dammit," the song that would become their first big hit, came to Mark when he was playing around on an acoustic guitar that was missing two strings. Having to skip over the missing strings created an interesting sound, and that sound became the distinctive "Dammit" riff.

Besides featuring this new material, *Dude Ranch* would also include re-recorded versions of two earlier songs that had been hard for fans to find. "Lemmings" had been available only on a seven-inch and blink-182 felt the song was too strong to limit it to fans with record players. "Degenerate" from *Buddha*, their rare cassette-only demo, was also included. That song, the tale of a boy, a cow, and a night spent in jail, still made blink-182 laugh, and they wanted as many people as possible to laugh with them.

"We just can't be too serious for too long. We always tried to get Mark [Trombino] to fuck around with us, but he just wasn't into it. We'd jump around naked, be retarded, and he'd just sit there. I guess he just didn't think we were funny. But that just made us try harder to get him to laugh." —Mark

It was so much better than being laughed at.

After their time at DML, blink-182 was ready to take what they had created to Big Fish. At the helm as producer was Mark Trombino. Blink-182 loved the work he had done with Jimmy Eat World, and as the former drummer of Drive Like Jehu, they knew he would understand the demands of musicians. He was good at his job, and took it seriously. Sometimes too seriously for Mark and Tom who tried desperately to get Trombino to laugh at them.

They may have tried, but blink-182 never really did get Mark Trombino to laugh with them. He was cool, but very quiet and very much his own person. He said little during the recording sessions except, "Let's try it again."

Tom: "It was a lot of fun, but we were in there for ten to twelve hours a day, doing things over and over until we got them right. Especially my vocals. I can't sing. I like the way everything sounds, but at the time I was taking an entire day to get one line done. I would get so pissed I was ready to break guitars."

Tom wasn't the only member of the band who was experiencing some recording difficulties. Shortly before the band had entered the studio, Scott had broken both of his heels. He spent time in a wheelchair, unable to put weight on his injured feet. Under doctor's orders, he could not play drums. Blink-182 had turned to Vandals tour drummer Brooks Wackerman to fill in for a few shows while Scott was recovering, but they didn't want another drummer recording the album.

71

72 The band contemplated delaying the recording, but were reluctant to do so. Luckily, Scott pushed himself, and had progressed from a wheelchair to crutches when it came time to record. He was not fully healed, but he felt well enough to record the drum tracks.

Mark, like Tom, had trouble with his vocals. Mark had made the mistake of writing the song "Dammit" just outside of his vocal range, requiring him to strain to sing it. Mark did take after take to get the song right. Listeners might notice the song's vocals have a scratchier sound to them; this was the result of hours of vocal strain that absolutely wrecked Mark's vocal cords.

After finishing "Dammit," the band left the studio for a Christmas show with the Vandals in Irvine. After the show and a few days off,

the band would return to the studio where Mark still had other vocal tracks to complete.

The Christmas show was going great when Mark felt his voice give out during one of the last songs. Tom noticed it as well, and promptly took over all of the vocals for the remainder of the show. But it was too late; Mark's voice was shot. He couldn't even speak. The combination of the days spent singing for the vocal tracks, Mark's constant smoking, his lack of vocal warm-ups, and the stress of straining to sing "Dammit" had killed his voice.

Although the band was scheduled to finish up their recording the following week, they were forced to cancel the studio time. It would be early 1997 before blink-182 would be able to wrap up *Dude Ranch*. But at least they got

some really different-sounding vocals on "Dammit" out of the whole experience.

Mark: "I actually like my voice a lot on 'Dammit.' It sounds really raw and cool. But it's not a technique I would recommend for getting a good vocal sound. You know, smoking, yelling, all that."

In fact, the experience scared Mark pretty seriously. He had never paid attention to taking care of his voice before. Now, suddenly he realized he had to. After a few more similar scares that resulted in cancelled shows and doctor visits, he got smart. He took care of his vocal cords and stopped smoking. You would too if the doctor shoved a big metal thing up through your nose and down your throat to look at growths on your vocal cords. Plus, Mark has always wanted to be able to sing like Whitney Houston, and now he is one step closer to that dream.

Even with these setbacks blink-182 was happy with their songs and happy with *Dude Ranch.* They had confidence in the quality of both the songs and the recording.

Tom: "I was extremely happy with that album. That was the first decent recording we had, everything sounded so amazing. Now, of course, there are things we'd like to change, but then, I thought it was perfect."

Mark: "I remember when we finished *Dude Ranch* I was so proud. That was the first time we could take the time and whatever to make a good record. I listen to it now, and I can hear things that I would like to change.

But I still think the songs are killer. I wouldn't change any of the songs, just the quality of the recording."

For some final touches, friend and Unwritten Law frontman Scott Russo donated a few vocal tracks to the album, and Mark Trombino let blink-182 play with his sound-effects machine to create a few stupid jokes to stick in between songs. With these details, the album was done.

Dude Ranch hit stores in June 1997, just as blink-182 was heading out on the Warped Tour. With fans spreading the news and with blink-182 touring nonstop, sales of the album were strong.

In January 1998, *Dude Ranch* went gold with 500,000 copies sold in the United States. The guys were dumbfounded; the band had been doing well, but no one had ever thought it would go this far.

Pushing the album on to gold status were blink-182's first two hit singles, "Dammit" and "Josie" and the truly blink-182-style videos that accompanied them.

The first single, "Dammit," broke in the summer of 1997, and instantly hit a chord with radio audiences. The song was added to the playlist at Los Angeles-based KROQ, the most influential alternative-format radio station in America. Soon, the song was being played all over the country. Mark began introducing himself to people as "that guy that wrote, 'duh nuh nuh nuh nuh duh nuh nuh nuh nuh, he fucked her.'"

"When I heard that we had gone gold, I was like, cool. It was a big thing, but it didn't really hit me. When we went to MCA, and they actually handed us a gold record, then I understood what was going on and it blew me away. Holy shit, look at this! A gold record! It was total acknowledgment for all of our hard work. It was awesome." —Tom

The success of the single also prompted the band to film a video. The band turned once again to Darren Doane.

Darren Doane worked well with blink-182 because he shared their sense of humor and was willing and able to roll with the punches. No matter how well planned out a blink-182 video shoot is, changes are bound to happen. As the shooting takes place, Mark and Tom suddenly start having these bright ideas. "Oh, dude, you know what would be so funny?" is a common phrase.

The "Dammit" shoot was no exception. When the band was shooting a scene in the theater lobby where manager Rick DeVoe was to fill in the background as a snack-bar attendant, they simply couldn't stop laughing at the personality Rick portrayed. They laughed so

hard they insisted that Darren find a way to work the character into more of the video. Eventually, Rick ended up stealing the show, being by far the funniest part of the video. And his character got the girl.

Tom: " 'Dammit' was such a squirrelly video. It was funny. I love that video."

With "Dammit" still attracting an audience, "Josie" was released as the second single. It, too, became a hit. The song is an account of all the traits Mark was looking for in a girlfriend. The song was named after a friend's dog, and the girlfriend was fictional, but the song still appealed to audiences. And again, blink would film a video to follow up their radio success.

The "Josie" video features TV star Alyssa Milano as the girl of Mark's affection. With

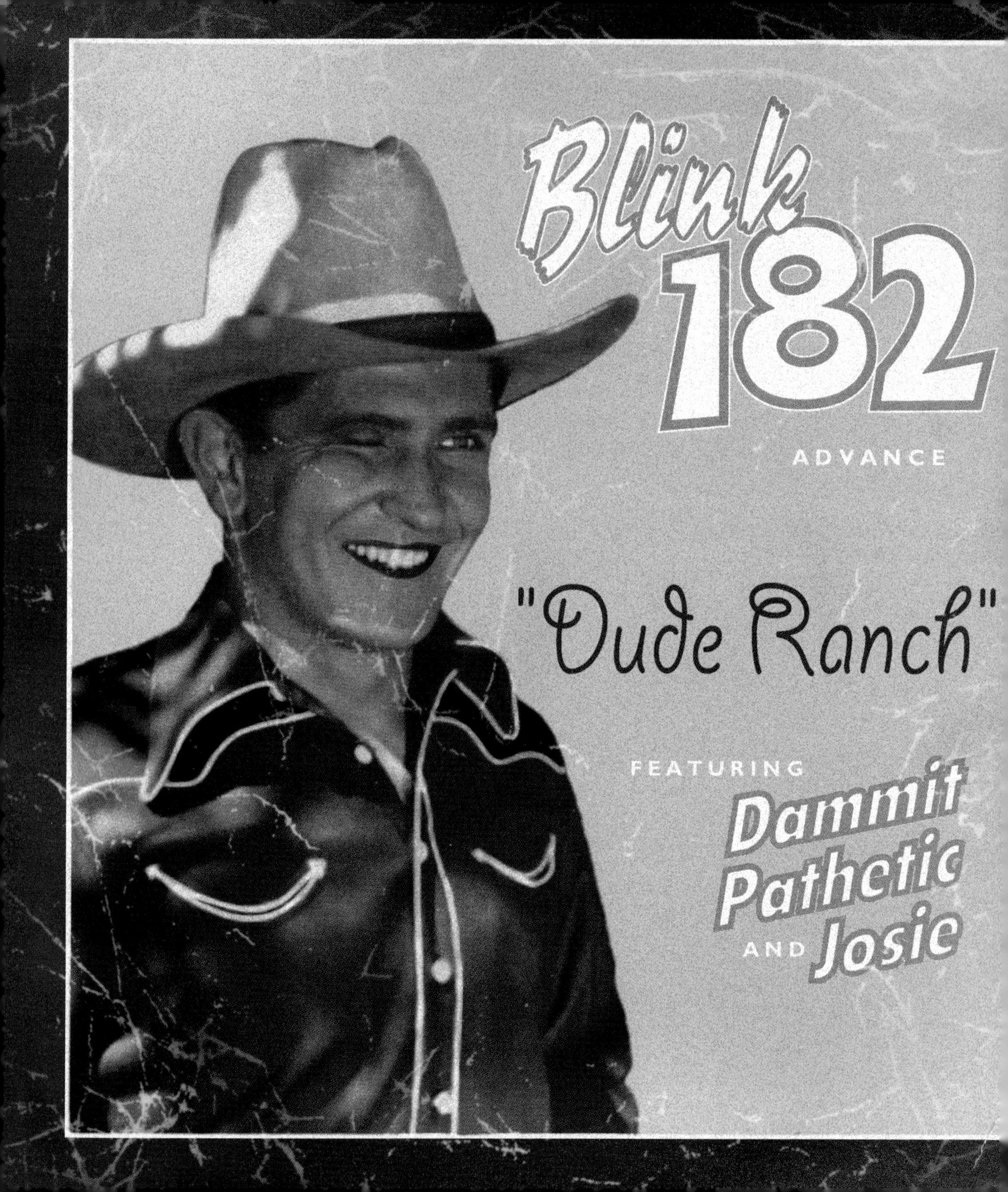
Blink
182
ADVANCE
"Dude Ranch"
FEATURING
Dammit
Pathetic
AND Josie

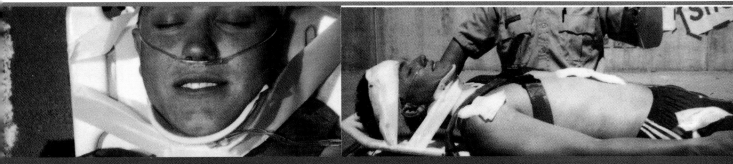

After finishing the 'Dammit' video, we kept hearing all these rumors. like the poster in the lobby of the theater is for a movie where the main character is castrated to let him hit the high notes, and that the new boyfriend guy that chases me is actually in gay porn. I don't know if those rumors are true or not, but I hope they're true. 'Cause that makes the video even more funny." —Mark

the exception of Tom, everyone on the set was stoked to work with the starlet. As preteen boys, they had lusted after her as "Samantha" on TV's *Who's the Boss?* Tom preferred Tony Danza.

Mark: "Alyssa—I call her by her first name—was really cool. She gave me her phone number. I felt really bad for her because she showed up on the set and it was just her and a bunch of perverted dudes who did nothing but stare at her breasts. They couldn't even help themselves."

Another highlight of the video, though less exciting than Alyssa Milano, was the infamous food-fight scene.

Mark: "The food fight scene was all done in one take because it was such a catastrophe, the place was destroyed. All those kids had

to sit around all day outside in the summer and, at the end of the day, they were rewarded by letting them nail us with tons of food. It was crazy. I got nailed with mashed potatoes right in the eye, and I seriously had mashed potatoes coming out of my eye for like three days. I'd think it was all gone, and then, squish, more would squeeze out. It was disgusting."

Despite the mashed-potato eye, both the band and their fans loved the video which quickly joined "M&Ms" and "Dammit" in the ranks of cult video favorites. Although none received extensive MTV play, all were viewed as incredible successes for the upstart band.

With a CD the band was proud of and that audiences loved, with two hit singles and two videos getting play on MTV, blink-182 was

78 accomplishing everything they had hoped to. Shit, they had a damn gold record! But the success wasn't just the by-product of a major-label release. Blink-182 was working hard. In between studio time and video shoots, the band was still doing what it had always done—touring, touring, touring.

Liza Remembers

Liza Bermingham has worked with blink-182 for years, beginning as a label rep for the band in Australia and eventually coming to America to work as an assistant manager for the band.

She recalls, "At a bowling alley for a retailer function, Mark and Tom started a food fight. My first clear memory of Mark is of him rubbing rice salad into his groin. Probably their first memory of me is taking them aside and very maternally and sternly demanding that they clean up their mess. That same night we had to talk Tom out of a tree and handcuff Rick DeVoe to a chair. But that's another story completely."

"On the Warped Tour in Australia in January 1998, blink-182 walked out on stage and started playing to 10,000 people and this was when I realized they had made it. When Tom started the first notes to "Dammit," all 10,000 kids screamed and threw their hands in the air. I was sitting behind Tom's amps. I got goosebumps, and Tom turned to look at me and mouth 'What the fuck?' All I could do was smile."

BLINK ★182★

"I'd rather date a girl who hates our band."
—Travis Barker, before meeting his girlfriend who, for the record, does not hate his band

8 By the time *Dude Ranch* was released, blink-182 was a band of seasoned travelers. They had toured the United States twice and had flown to Australia and Alaska. They thought they were tough, but they hadn't seen shit yet. Beginning in the summer of 1997, blink-182 would enter such an extended period of touring that the hard realities of living on the road for so long would eventually change the face of the band.

In 1996, blink-182 had played a handful of dates on the Warped Tour, a lifestyle tour promoting skateboarding and punk-rock music. In 1997, they would play every date of the tour worldwide. As far as both sides were concerned, blink-182 and the Warped Tour were a perfect match. The subcultures the tour catered to were the subcultures

that blink-182 had grown up in. The tour referred to itself as "punk-rock summer camp" and became more of a roving party than anything else. The bands became friends, people would jump on a bus at one city and ride for the rest of the tour, and who could forget the traditional aftershow barbecues.

Tom: "The Warped Tour is really more of a traveling-band barbecue. You hang out with the other bands all day, you play your set, and then hang out again. And it's awesome because you end up with like a hundred people—everyone on the tour—as your friends. If something happens, all those people have your back, they're willing to fight for you. Which is good for our band because people everywhere want to kick our ass."

Mark: "You make friends with everyone, it doesn't matter what band they're in. There's no rock-star attitudes, no bullshit."

The tour, while fun, was also hot, dirty, and uncomfortable. It takes place in the middle of the summer and the shows are often outside, forcing the bands to play in the hot sun in 100+ degree weather with dirt, dust, and/or grass being kicked up by the energetic fans. The drives between shows are long. Most bands on the Warped Tour travel on buses, allowing the bands to sleep during the often overnight drives to the next city. In 1996, blink-182 had not been able to afford the expense of a bus and had to travel by van. After taking turns driving all night, the band would arrive at the venue first thing in the morning. They would unload the equipment, watch the show, play, load the equipment, and immediately leave to drive to the next city. For weeks, the band lived out of their van, without benefit of showers or sleep. In the middle of the tour, the possibility of spending a night in a hotel grew even bleaker when the entire profits of the tour— $6000—were stolen.

Mark: "Our roadie went into town with some kid to buy equipment—guitar strings, drum heads, etc. He left the cashbox with all of the money in the car. After shopping around for a while, he came out to get the money and, of course, the car had been broken into and the cashbox taken. It was absolutely devastating. It was the worst thing that could've happened. It was our

most successful tour up to then—we were looking forward to breaking even, and maybe even having a little bit of spending money left over. Instead, all of a sudden, we were in Canada in the middle of a tour, and we had no money to our names at all. It was horrible."

But whatever the amount of discomfort, the good parts of the Warped Tour far outweigh the bad. The true hallmark of the Warped Tour is the legions of kids who turn out year after year and the high-caliber bands that attract them. When Kevin Lyman, founder of the Warped Tour, and Darrel Eaton, now blink-182's booking agent, gave blink-182 a slot on the Warped Tour, they gave them the opportunity to play in front of thousands of kids every day on the same stage with bands like Lagwagon, NOFX, and Social Distortion. The exposure did enormous things for the band.

The Warped Tour exposed blink-182 to more than just American audiences. They also went overseas to Europe, Australia, and Japan. All in all, blink-182 would be traveling with the Warped Tour for four months at the end of 1997. In between the Warped Tour dates, blink-182 was touring on their own as well. In late 1997 and early 1998, the band would be on the road for nine months straight, coming home for merely days at a time before striking out on the next tour. Not to sound like *Behind the Music* or anything, but the exhausting schedule was beginning to take its toll on the band.

Tom: "I remember the first time we went to Australia, the drummer from Pennywise was so bummed, all he wanted to do was go home. I totally didn't get it. I just kept thinking, what's this guy's problem? He's touring the world with his band, and he wants to go home? But he's been doing it for a long, long time, and I was brand-new at it. When all you do is tour, it's hard. You get superhomesick. I totally understand where he was coming from now. When we did our longest tour stretch, it was right when I started dating my fiancée. We were all new and in love, and I had to leave. It was just, 'Hey, I'll see you in nine months.' It was really hard."

All three band members were desperate for a break. They wanted a chance to be home where everything was familiar, where their

friends were just down the street. Mark, Tom, and Scott were living in a weird world where the only constant was that everything would be different from one day to the next. Overworked and overtired, the three friends began to argue. Tension formed in the band, they needed time apart.

It wasn't all bad; the shows were steadily growing larger. The tours were amazing and the kind that blink-182 had always wanted the opportunity to play. As always, when blink-182 took the stage, all the hardship of life on the road disappeared and the fun of playing a live show took over.

Mark: "Touring is hard, but playing almost never is. You can have the shittiest day ever—awful drive, you hate the guys in your band, whatever. But when you step on stage

Hidden Extras In Blink-182 Videos

You may have seen all of the blink-182 videos, but have you seen all there is to be seen in those videos? Here are some extra points of interest you may want to note:

- All three bandmate's bedrooms in "M&Ms" are bedrooms in Mark's mom's house, the outside of which is not shown in the video.

- At the very end of the video, when the camera pans out over the empty club, a lone figure can be seen in the club. It's Anne, Mark's sister, wearing an alien mask. Seriously.

- In "Dammit," Mark accidentally trips the new boyfriend character when he stops to do his little jig mid-chase.

- The wacky concession-stand employee is none other than blink-182 manager Rick DeVoe.

- After Mark pulls Tom's pants down at the concession stand in "Dammit", Scott turns to Tom and mouths, "Hey your pants fell down".

- Later, when the band is playing, Tom mouths to Mark, "I love you."

- In "Josie" the woman who plays Mark's mom is actually director Darren Doane's mother.

- Though not necessarily visible, there are *Stars Wars* references sprinkled throughout the "Josie" set. Both Mark and one member of the crew are huge fans of the movie. One reference is a school election poster supporting "Grand Mof Tarkin for School President."

- The khakis-clad dancers in "What's My Age Again" were not told that the band would be running through naked. The surprise on their faces is real.

- Manager Rick DeVoe can be seen again at the end of "All The Small Things" as the naked man in the crowd of fans.

you remember how awesome it is to play music for a living, and most of that goes away. But then as soon as you step off the stage, it all comes right back."

Blink-182 had always been first and foremost a live band, and they never lost their love of playing to an audience. A good show could erase a week's worth of tension. What frustrations they couldn't relieve on stage they turned into music. "Adam's Song" was written based partly on the loneliness that Mark experienced in these hard unending days of touring. With some time off, the band would be fine. They loved their "jobs," they just needed a vacation.

With that vacation still months away, Scott's mood darkened. Always quiet, he grew even more quiet and remote. He disagreed with

Mark and Tom on many issues, and the band sank into a period of prolonged arguing. At one time the band had always been a united front and had stood as friends. Now, they were sick of each other. As often as possible, they tried to separate themselves to relieve the tension they all felt in the band.

The tension came to a head in February 1998 as the band embarked on yet another tour. It was SnoCore, a winter version of the Warped Tour that had blink-182 sharing a stage with Primus and the Aquabats. Blink-182 was enjoying more success than they ever had before. Still, the tour did not go well for the band.

Tom: "SnoCore was the worst tour ever. It was cold and the shows weren't that good. Everything was too expensive for the kids,

and it really wasn't our crowd. And there was terrible band drama. It was pretty shitty."

By then, Scott would have little or nothing to do with his band, disappearing before and after shows and appearing only to play the set. But he would not discuss the situation with his band. He kept his distance and the entire band suffered in silence.

Mark: "I remember just wanting that tour to be over. It was a definite low point, the worst tour we ever did. Everything about that tour was dark—the weather, the mood. Everything."

Still, it was hard to be down when the band was doing better than ever. Following the end of SnoCore was a short minitour along the western coast. Again, the Aquabats were playing with blink-182. The West Coast,

especially Southern California, has always been among blink-182's favorite places to play, and this minitour was no exception. The shows were large and the crowds energetic. The minitour was an undeniable success. To top it off, the final show on the brief stint was a headlining show at the Palladium in Hollywood, California. For years, blink-182 had dreamed of playing the Palladium, a venue that had hosted some of music history's greatest acts. Now, they were finally seeing that dream come true.

Mark: "To me, playing the Palladium was as big as anything else we had done with the band. I mean, the Palladium was where all the big bands played. I had seen my heroes play the Palladium. I remember thinking that if I ever got to play the Palladium, that I would have totally made it. That would be

the best I could ever do. And holy shit, here we were, about to play the Palladium."

The show was sold out. Blink-182 could not believe they had sold out the Palladium. Once again, they had reached a musical milestone and blown it out of the water.

The band's ability to enjoy this moment of triumph was short-lived, however, when Scott announced to his band that he was leaving the tour. He would return in time for the show at the Palladium but that was all he could promise. Mark and Tom were stunned. They were about to play some of the biggest shows of their career and suddenly they were left without a drummer. Two drummers had filled in for Scott in the past, but neither was available on such short notice. Luckily, Travis Barker, the drummer for the Aquabats,

stepped up and offered his services. For the remainder of the minitour, Travis played drums for blink-182 until Scott returned to the stage at the Palladium. With no chance to practice with the band, Travis learned the songs in forty-five minutes.

Tom: "I'm not sure what that says about me as a songwriter. Either I write really easy songs, or he's a really talented drummer. I prefer to believe the latter."

Whatever the reason, Travis played perfectly.

Travis: "The hardest part for me was that I wasn't too familiar with their first album. So it was challenging, but fun. Filling in on those shows was definitely fun. I had a good time."

Mark and Tom were impressed. And thank-

ful. Without Travis, blink-182 would have had to cancel shows all along the West Coast.

Scott did return, but the feeling was still wrong. Mark and Tom felt Scott's heart was in the wrong place. Scott found himself increasingly uneasy.

Scott: "I think Mark and Tom are better suited for what they are doing. It didn't fit me. I was always fighting for a different direction and that conflict eventually led to a split."

Without more than a short break, the band headed off to Australia for a few weeks of shows. The band was tired and stressed, but they had audiences around the world waiting to see them play, and blink-182 was not about to let them down. Traditionally, the

Australian audiences went off, and blink-182 was looking forward to a string of good shows Down Under.

Unfortunately, while the audiences did go off, the tension in the band did not pass. The arguments grew worse. It was time to accept that the band had changed permanently.

Following the tour in Australia, the band finally had time to rest. The band hoped this break would help relieve the bad feelings among the three members. It didn't. After meetings and phone calls and other earnest attempts to keep the original lineup intact, the band accepted the inevitable. It just wasn't possible to keep going the way things were. Unable to resolve their differences, the original blink-182 line-up split.

While Scott moved on to pursue other life

avenues, Mark and Tom continued on with blink-182. For a drummer, they turned again to Travis Barker.

Soft-spoken Travis was just about the best drummer Mark and Tom had ever seen. He was renowned throughout the music scene. He was also a full-time member of the Aquabats, but they hoped he might be willing to make a change. Travis had played perfectly with the band, and his personality was a good match as well. Travis and the band had become tight friends over the past few months they had toured together. He wasn't as loud or as rude as Mark or Tom, but the guys got along. As it turned out, Travis was as interested in playing with blink-182 as blink-182 was in having him join the band.

Travis: "I had been a fan of blink-182 for a few years. I thought Mark and Tom were superfunny. When they asked me to join the band, I was excited. It was an opportunity. Being asked to play in the band, it was good."

And so, in the summer of 1998, Travis Barker became an official member of blink-182. With hardly a transition period, he was thrown into the band's hectic schedule, learning songs and band dynamics at the same time.

Tom: "As far as music goes, Travis fit in instantaneously. Personality wise, it took a little longer. He wasn't used to us, and we weren't used to him. It's different to have a new person in your band, it changes things.

It just took a while for us to understand each other. You know, all of a sudden we had this new person in the band, and for him, all of a sudden he was in this new band. We tried to make him feel at home, but in reality, we were all strangers. But we've never had any gnarly arguments or vibes or anything. And now, things are so much better. It's good."

Though Travis Barker was a newcomer to blink-182, he was certainly no stranger to music. Music was a constant presence for Travis growing up. By the time he was four years old, he had his first drum kit. And while drums were his musical initiation, his musical education was not limited to that one instrument. Travis played drums for a few years, and then left the drum kit to study piano, guitar, even singing. While other kids in the neighborhood were skateboarding and running around outside, Travis was often inside taking lessons on one instrument or another. No lesson that day? Time for practice. A lot of the time Travis would have preferred to be outside with the other kids, but the lessons were important to his parents who had to work extra hard for the money to provide them. Her son's musical education was especially important to Travis's mother who was often the driving force behind his studies. Tragically, she was diagnosed with cancer and died, just as Travis started high school. Before her death, she implored her son to follow his true talent and see where it could take him. With his mother's words

88 fresh in his mind, Travis threw himself whole-heartedly into the drums. He played in his high school band, continued taking lessons, practiced every single day, and eventually became one of the best drummers around.

While Travis's ability is by no means limited to any particular musical genre (Travis can play just about anything—trust us), punk has always been the style that captured his imagination. Well, punk and hip-hop. But that's beside the point. It was punk music that Travis loved to play, and when he turned his attention to joining a band, it was in the punk world that Travis began his journey. Outside of his more formal drum education, Travis took his mother's words to heart and turned his talent into his life's career. Before blink-182 found him, Travis played in Feeble, a Fontana, CA, band. From there Travis

moved on to the Aquabats, where as Baron von Tito he recorded an album with the band and toured extensively. But even after signing on with the blink-182 boys, Travis continued to play with other bands, including a stint with punk-rock legends The Vandals following the recording of the drum tracks for *Enema of the State*. Travis just can't get enough of music. Which is good for blink-182. Travis's talent, range, and drive have been significant contributions to the band, helping them reach undreamed of heights.

Travis would tour with the band for the remainder of 1998, playing sold-out shows across America on the Poo-Poo Pee-Pee tour. Then, in January 1999, he entered the studio with the band and helped to usher in a new era for blink-182.

90

Worldwide Sales

- Canada: 4 x platinum

- Australia: 3 x platinum

- New Zealand: 2 x platinum

- Italy: 2 x platinum

- Germany: gold

- UK: gold

- Austria: gold

- Switzerland: gold

- Mexico: gold

- Indonesia: gold

- Philippines: gold

> ## "You only get a few years to act like an immature bastard and have a good time and get paid a ridiculous amount of money for it."
> —Mark Hoppus

9 In January 1999, blink-182 began recording a brand-new album. Again, two years had passed since they had last been in the studio. The band was anxious to record new songs, but in the tumultuous period that had just passed, the band had lost track of time. Suddenly, the new album loomed before them.

Blink-182 returned to DML Studios to write the new songs. With Travis driving down from Riverside every day, the band dug in and came out two weeks later, satisfied with the results.

Don Lithgow, owner and operator of DML Studios remembers, "I've been working with these guys forever. So it's just like friends coming in. I bust their balls. I love 'em. They're great guys. This last time they came

in was different than their other sessions— girls hanging around outside, calling their friends on cell phones. All the kids wanted autographs. But the guys are the same, not touched by that whole rock-star thing. They'd unlock the doors and let kids into the studio, which most bands would never do."

MCA had faith in the band, too, and gave blink-182 their first serious recording budget.

After writing and recording demos for the songs, the band headed to Los Angeles to record the drums at Chick Corea's Mad Hatter Studios. Travis tore through the drums, finishing all of his tracks in only a few days.

Travis: "I just went in there and got it done. You know, it was pretty easy. I knew what I wanted to do."

"There was all this pressure on us to make a good album, because *Dude Ranch* had gone gold. People kept asking us if we were scared about recording a follow-up. We didn't even think about that, we just wrote good songs." —Mark

92 To record this record, blink-182 turned to punk-rock producer Jerry Finn. Blink-182 decided to bring him on board for the new album after recording "Mutt" with him for the *American Pie* soundtrack. Jerry had made the song sound phenomenal. Jerry was also well known for his work with great bands like Green Day. He was definitely the man they wanted for their full-length CD.

Tom: "I knew we'd made the right choice with Jerry when I heard the first tracks that we recorded. Just those tracks without mixing or anything sounded awesome. We knew this was going to be the best thing we ever did."

Mark: "Jerry is first an awesome, awesome human being, and then he's an incredible producer. He grew up playing in punk-rock bands. He knows punk-rock music. He knows what works in songs. He lives music, it's all he cares about, and he can listen to a song and tell what it needs in a second. He made *Enema* sound awesome."

It wasn't just musically that the band worked well with Jerry. They had also found the producer that fit their personalities. Almost a little too well. The band had so much fun recording with Jerry that there were days where very little work was accomplished.

Tom: "Jerry Finn is a shit talker. He is the only guy I've ever met who knows all the answers to the millionaire questions, to any trivia thing ever. He knows all this shit, but he only uses it to down on other people. It's superfunny, and you just laugh all the time while he ruins these other people and other

bands, while he makes these horrible jokes. He was the perfect combination with us. But we'd walk into the studio and he'd say, 'Want to get to work?' and we'd say, 'No'. So we'd just do something else. God, it was funny."

Mark: "Recording can get pretty monotonous, but at least we could laugh with Jerry. A pretty typical day would involve multiple takes for one part of one song, and then everyone would get naked and jump on Jerry."

Tom: "We choose never to work with any-one else again."

When all was said and done, blink-182 was enormously proud of the album they had made.

Tom: "When it was done, we were so stoked. It was like a masterpiece for our band. Whether or not people liked it, we liked it. We felt like Mozart; of course we realized later we were more like Liberace."

Mark: "*Enema* was the very first time I listened to one of our albums all the way through and said, that's exactly the way I want it to sound."

Jerry Finn was impressed with the results of his and the band's work as well. "I thought the album was good when we finished it. Now, after living with it, I'm really proud. They are all phenomenal songs; there are no skip-over songs. At first I thought it was just a good blink-182 album, now I feel like it's a great anybody album."

Every night on the Mark, Tom, and Travis Show tour, blink-182 would coax the thousands of kids in the audience into chanting, "Larry has herpes" every time guitar tech Larry Palmer would walk on stage to fix Mark's or Tom's guitars.

In his defense to the herpes accusations, Larry says, "Everyone asks me if the jokes make me mad. It's really pretty harmless. There's a lot worse things said on stage. Really, it's all just part of the show. It's a big game, and I'm game for it. Nothing is sacred with them. It's all in good fun."

96 Those who worked on the album were not the only ones to whom it appealed. The album, dubbed *Enema of the State,* was an immediate hit. It shipped gold to stores and went platinum only a few months later. Sales have now risen to almost six million worldwide.

Travis: "When we went platinum, it was hard to believe, of course, but I don't know. I really felt like we deserved it. I was very happy."

The album spawned a string of hit singles, including "What's My Age Again?" "All the Small Things," and "Adam's Song." These songs were bigger hits than anyone in the blink camp had anticipated, crossing over into Top-40 radio format.

Videos for all three songs dominated MTV's *Total Request Live,* with "All The Small

Things" being retired before it fell off the list. The videos were typical blink-182 humor.

"What's My Age Again?" directed by Marcos Siega, features the band running naked through the streets of Los Angeles, crashing commercials, and taking a naked walk through the daily news. The video quickly gave the band a reputation for nakedness that has plagued them ever since.

Tom: "You know, when we were filming the video for 'What's My Age Again?' the whole naked thing was only funny for like ten minutes. Then, I was the guy standing naked on the side of the street in Los Angeles with cars driving by giving me the finger and shit. It's funny watching the video now, but at the time, it stopped being funny ten minutes in, and it definitely wasn't funny three days into it."

"All the Small Things," the most successful of blink-182's videos, parodies boy bands and pop-music videos.

Mark: " 'All the Small Things' gave me a chance to show off my dance moves. Actually, what I remember most about the ATST video shoot was meeting the girl who is now my wife on the set."

Travis: "I don't really dance, and they made me do some pretty idiotic things in that video. I'm kinda shy when it comes to stuff like that, so it was kinda hard for me. But looking back on it, I love the video."

Tom: "The video for 'All the Small Things' is awesome. Most importantly, we had a chance to laugh at other bands instead of being the band being laughed at. Though I

guess, technically, people are still laughing at us. . . . I don't know. Shit."

No matter who was laughing at whom, the video was a smash hit, even snagging the band a Moon Man for Best Group Video at the 2000 MTV Video Music Awards.

With massive radio and video play, blink-182 attracted legions of new fans. To satisfy the crowds, blink-182 embarked on two arena tours beginning with the Loserkids Tour in the fall of 1999. This was the band's first large-venue tour, and on top of it, they were playing to mostly sold-out audiences.

Tom: "Loserkids, our first arena tour, was my favorite tour by far. It was amazing, because it was the first time we'd ever done anything that big. I felt like a success story. It was awesome."

Mark: "Every single night you forget how big an arena really is. Then you walk out on stage and see all the kids, and it's like Holy Shit. It's awesome."

After Loserkids, the ball continued to roll for the band, with sales continuing and singles topping the charts. In the summer of 2000, blink-182 traveled the world with the "Mark, Tom, and Travis Show," a full arena tour with an old drive-in movie theme. This time out, blink-182 was playing the largest venues available, and yet again, the shows were almost entirely sold out.

Mark: "When we sold out the Great Western Forum in Los Angeles, I walked off stage and just sat there. I couldn't believe my band had done that. I was completely overwhelmed, and all emotional and shit,

because so few bands ever get to do that. I had never thought that we would do something like that, and we did. I remember exactly what that felt like."

To celebrate the success of the tour, which was so big even Satan was known to make appearances, blink-182 released a limited edition live album called *The Enema Strikes Back: The Mark, Tom, and Travis Show* featuring performances from the Mark, Tom, and Travis Show tour. Remaining true to their live show, the CD even features snippets of blink-182's infamous between-song dialogue. Understandably, these snippets earned the band a Parental Advisory sticker.

Blink-182's success is undeniable, and they are amazed at the distance their band has come over the years. Starting out in Tom's

garage eight years before, the band had hoped simply to play real shows, and now they are playing arenas. But first and foremost, the band's primary motivation is to have fun while playing good music.

Mark: "Blink-182 has never really had any goals. We wanted to make it, we wanted to get big if we could, get played on the radio, make videos, do all that. But our one goal really was to write good songs, to be a good band, and if people come to the shows, cool, if people buy the albums, good. We just want to still be writing songs that keep us around for a little bit longer."

Tom: "Everyone always asks us if we have a philosophy, what our band is supposed to mean. We're just trying to have a good time, trying to make ourselves laugh, and make

the kids laugh. We don't have a bigger message than that."

Travis: "I'm happy with how things are going in the band. I really like that the band is getting into more music, more than just what we were listening to a few years ago. I want to see the band keep growing that way. I like that."

Beyond the band, all three members of blink-182 have homes and dogs and significant others, not necessarily in that order. Their success has allowed them to branch out into other areas.

Mark and Tom launched an internet company called Loserkids.com that sells surf, skate, and snowboarding gear as well as music. The idea was to make these items accessible to kids who don't have the luxury of living in

areas like Southern California where cool stores can be found on nearly every corner.

Travis, too, has reached into the retail world, opening a store in Riverside, California called Famous Stars and Straps. The store specializes in custom belts and buckles, but sells a wide array of other cool merchandise from clothing to Marilyn Monroe posters. Unfortunately, the storefront was shut down by the city, but FSAS is far from gone. FSAS products are being carried by other retailers and are also available directly from the Famous Stars and Straps web page.

Travis: "Famous Stars and Straps is my baby company. It's almost like the band in a way. You know, I get to watch it grow from something small, and I know that it's my work that's making it grow."

Besides running FSAS, Travis also offers drum lessons and will soon be adding Guitar Center drum clinics to his list of activities.

Travis: "The drum lessons I just do for fun. I actually charge less than most teachers do, but it's fun."

In 1998, Mark tried his hand at music management by taking on an upstart band called Fenix tx. When his own band's career took off in a big way, he stepped down to a co-management position, sharing responsibilities with blink-182's own manager, Rick DeVoe.

And in addition to all of that, the members of blink-182 have been known to make an appearance or two on the big screen.

All three members of the band appeared in the 1999 hit movie *American Pie*. From

there, Mark and Tom made other brief film appearances. Tom had a small role in *Idle Hands,* where he played a fast-food worker, and not too convincingly.

Mark: "Tom definitely deserves as Oscar for his work in *Idle Hands.* The way he nods his head and says, 'All right'—I believed it! It was pure genius."

Later, Mark and Tom appeared together in the CBS movie *Shake, Rattle, and Roll* as surf musicians Jan and Dean, as well as recording a version of the duo's hit, "Deadman's Curve" for the TV movie's soundtrack.

Eventually, Mark and Tom would like to be more involved in the movie industry. The two have worked on and off on a screenplay for a movie tentatively titled *Pranksters,* where

104 two friends try to out-prank each other. It's a familiar story to the two close friends. Another movie, a pet project of blink-182 video director Marcos Siega to star the two blink-182 frontmen, has been briefly put on hold due to time constraints. But all parties are eager to see the project move forward.

In the meantime, Mark, Tom, and Travis are enjoying the results of years of hard work and dreaming. The band has a new album to be released in the summer of 2001. Again, blink-182 brushes off any pressure of making a follow-up album. They're concentrating instead on being the best blink-182 they can be, picking out new tunes on acoustic guitars until all those around them are sick, calling each other with hilarious new album titles, and just being the same stupid bunch of loserkids they always have been. Blink-182 has always come so naturally; they're not really thinking about it.

Tom: "I just wanna see a UFO, really."

MTV Video Music Awards

In September 2000, blink-182 was nominated for three MTV Video Music Awards, including Best Group Video, Video of the Year, and Best Pop Video. All three members were anxious, not knowing what, if anything, they would walk away with.

"We were really hoping that we would win Best Group. We knew we didn't even have a chance for Video of the Year, and we didn't even really want to win Best Pop. And everyone kept telling us different things. Like, you're the last performer—you didn't win anything and they gave you that slot to make up for it. And, you're the last performer, you had to have won something. They wouldn't close out the show with someone who didn't win anything. I was nervous, but I just kept reminding myself that it didn't matter if we won anything. Having an award wasn't going to change anything. You know, we never started a band thinking we were going to win awards," Mark remembers.

Travis had a feeling they were going to win. "I got up to go to the restroom and this MTV guy almost tackled me. He kept telling me I had to be in my seat. He followed me to the restroom, and made sure I hurried right back to my seat. They were getting ready to announce the Best Group, so I figured we must have won. Why else would they have wanted me to be in my seat. But it was still cool."

Travis's feeling about winning Best Group was right. They did win. And Mark's feelings about the band's other two nominations also were right. The band did not take home either of those awards, a score Mark noted when he taped the message "1 of 3" on his bass cabinet during the bands little people and pyrotechnic filled closing performance. In addition to their award, blink-182 received a standing ovation for the show's finale. It was a good night.

Tom explains, "Winning the Moon Man was like getting our first gold record times ten. I never thought our band would do anything like that. No way. I almost can't believe it. But I have this big silver space man sitting on my fireplace to prove it."

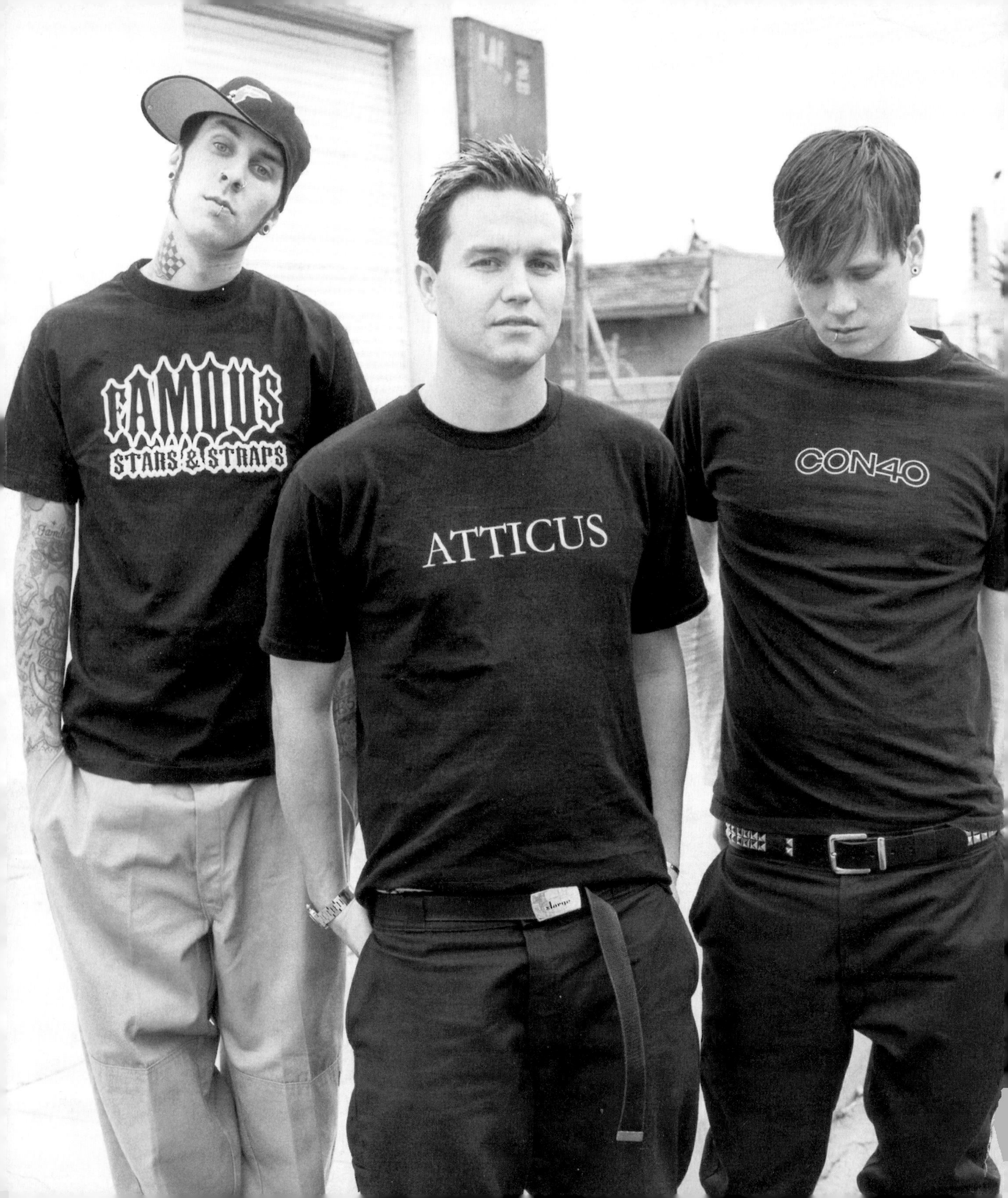
FAMOUS
STARS & STRAPS
ATTICUS
CON40